CUT FLOWERS

FOR TOBY, WILLOW, LILAC & AUGUST COURTAULD

FORBES, GEORGE, VIOLET & SOMERS ELWORTHY

THE LAND GARDENERS
CUT FLOWERS

BRIDGET ELWORTHY & HENRIETTA COURTAULD

PHOTOGRAPHY

CLIVE NICHOLS, CLARE RICHARDSON, MIGUEL FLORES-VIANNA,

ANDREW MONTGOMERY, HUGO RITTSON-THOMAS

& THE LAND GARDENERS

Thames & Hudson

10 - FOREWORD by Miranda Brooks

₁₅ THE LAND GARDENERS

20 - Designing Gardens   24 - It All Begins in the Soil

₂₉ A FLORAL HISTORY

₄₁ CREATION OF A CUTTING GARDEN

46 - The Walled Garden   52 - The Cutting Garden

56 - The Dahlia and Tulip Borders   60 - The Perennial Borders   64 - The Pond Walk

64 - The Orchard   64 - The Church Walk

₆₉ THE FLOWER ROOM

74 - Gathering   80 - Preparing   82 - Potting Up   86 - To Market

₉₃ A YEAR OF FLOWERS

95 - Spring   115 - Summer   139 - Autumn   159 - Winter

YOUR CUT-FLOWER GARDEN 181

Making Flower Beds - 182   Protecting the Beds - 182   Edging the Beds - 183

Paths - 183   Compost - 184   Liquid Feeds - 186

Green Manures - 188   The Potting Shed - 192   Under Cover - 194

Staking and Supports - 196   Collecting Seed - 198

Our Favourite Tools - 200

GROWING CUT FLOWERS 203

Roses - 206   Peonies - 210   Dahlias - 214   Bulbs and Corms - 220   Tulips - 226

Annuals - 230   Biennials - 236   Perennials - 238   Foliage - 242

Climbers - 244   Trees and Shrubs - 246

RESOURCES - 252

ACKNOWLEDGEMENTS - 254

Compost and Constance Spry pull equal weight in the world created by The Land Gardeners. Having first learned of them through Instagram, and seduced by their dahlias, I finally met the girls at Wardington Manor: a house that seems to have recreated its past, and found the owners of its choosing. The manor – Jacobean meets Arts and Crafts – is a rambling composition of elaborate plasterwork, dusky rooms, chintz, flowers in pots, flowers in buckets and flowers on display.

The Land Gardeners, in Le Laboureur blues, or tweeds like their Land Girl predecessors, appear to be digging for England. Old garden walks and former paddocks are once again planted for cutting, with every square inch pressed into production and nothing spared, so that they can once again, in Constance Spry fashion, supply London rooms with the freshness of hedgerow flowers, and the reality of the country and its seasons. These two are serious: their supply is rooted in their trial compost beds, the microbe-rich soil being their passion, and the cultivated soil of old walled gardens their design speciality.

Visually, the garden is the star of this book, but don't just look at the pictures, for it is the information – from soil preparation to planting combinations and staking techniques, even the utilization of one's bathtub for plant teas – that is so absorbing, and makes this book invaluable.

Teamwork and vision, needed to fuel their enterprises, is something I admire in The Land Gardeners, and rather covet. I am signing up for their next soil workshop, and this lovely book has certainly increased my determination.

Miranda Brooks, New York

The Land Gardeners

A shared love of learning about plants, soil health and the creation of beautiful, productive, truly alive gardens inspired us to start The Land Gardeners in 2012. We wanted to connect with our gardens and encourage others to do the same.

We had met years before at our children's nursery school in London, talking plants to avoid talking play dates at the nursery door. Although brought up on opposite sides of the world (Bridget in New Zealand and Henrietta in England) we had so much in common: we had both spent our childhoods playing in the garden, then trained and worked as lawyers, before becoming obsessed with plants and changing tack to study garden design and horticulture.

In the early days we spent hours in cafes together scribbling our dreams on paper tablecloths – the beginnings of The Land Gardeners. We knew we wanted to grow, to learn; we wanted to spend our time in gardens humming with life, and we wanted to laugh. We craved beauty, but grounded in the reality of mud under our nails. We wanted to learn more, to work with nature, not against it; supporting, not controlling it.

Nothing is ever straightforward with us. We started running our design business, specialising in the restoration of old walled gardens and the creation of new productive gardens, while also researching soil health when we stumbled across the idea of growing cut flowers. Ordering flowers from London florist Scarlet & Violet, we were surprised to find that the owner, Vic Brotherson, longed to supply billowing, natural, autumnal blooms like cosmos and dinner plate dahlias, but no one was growing them. The flower markets supplied boxes of carefully graded, imported flowers, but not the blowsy, wild and gloriously imperfect blooms of garden-grown plants.

In an impulsive moment, we agreed to start growing these flowers at Bridget's home, Wardington Manor, in Oxfordshire, reawakening its history of cut-flower production. Growing flowers was a perfect way for us to put into practice the knowledge that we were accumulating about soil and plants. It has been a helter-skelter journey, rather chaotic and impulsive; we are endlessly seduced by delicious blooms in the winter, over-ordering seeds and bulbs on a monumental scale and then experiencing an overwhelming sense of unease when our parcels arrive. It has been exhausting – blooming cut flowers don't wait for anyone – but it has been incredibly rewarding and we have learned so much on the way.

This is a book about our story and a visual diary of all we have learned. It is not a comprehensive 'how to' book, as this has been done so skilfully already by Sarah Raven in England and by Erin Benzakein in the US, whose incredible knowledge and books have taught us much of what we know. It is instead a book of ideas and inspiration – whether you are wanting to pick from your existing garden, create new dedicated cut-flower beds or even start growing for a cut-flower business. We take you through a year of flowers in the garden, showing you what to do and what to gather season by season. We talk about our favourite plants and how we grow them, sharing what we have learned to help you create your own cutting garden.

When designing gardens for clients, we always ask them to create a moodboard, collecting images and other things that fill them with joy: fabrics, flowers, music, scent, art and so on. This is part of our own Land Gardeners moodboard that we have on our studio wall.

the beautiful
in a Pretty
beautiful
white
Chiffon

Designing Gardens

Growing cut flowers is not the only thing that fills our busy weeks. When not gardening at Wardington, we spend our time running our design business from our studio at the bottom of Henrietta's garden. We love to feel the path of time in any garden, researching its history, quietly working with what we find and developing it. Just as we have re-awakened the garden at Wardington, so we find it fascinating to rediscover a garden's past and breathe new life into its bones.

We have tried to tread gently at Wardington, clothing the underlying structure of the gardens with ebullient planting, softening it and allowing nature to bring it to life. Nature lures you in, teaches you and takes you beyond your imagination, with its unpredictability and changing seasons. For us, a garden is all about atmosphere; it may be beautiful or functional, but it is the spirit of a garden that will induce you to fall under its spell. Working with our clients on how they want to feel in their garden is always our starting point. The results are gloriously individual: from a garden to free the soul in Oxfordshire where our client wants to dance around her garden in leg warmers listening to Kate Bush to a productive garden in the Umbrian hills where the owner dreams of gathering baskets of pomegranates, vegetables and herbs to feed long tables of family and friends or a walled garden in Hampshire to evoke 1940s glamour, think Rita Hayworth in *Gilda*, a garden full of blowsy blooms and satin silk peonies.

Throughout our journey we have remained passionate advocates of the productive garden: the joy of gathering and connecting. We are continually looking for ways to weave elements of productivity into clients' gardens, whether we are restoring an old walled garden, planting an orchard or even adding wild roses and hips to an existing hedgerow. Our work as growers supports our work as designers. Each year we trial new varieties of flowers, herbs, fruit and vegetables and share what we learn with our clients.

Underlying our two businesses is our obsession with soil, which is fundamental to the success of our cut flowers and our designs. We spend much of our week looking at ways of improving the health of our soil to ensure the resilience of our flowers and gardens. We try to work with the force of nature that flows through a garden, the energy it emanates, its rhythms and the life it supports: the goal is not perfection, but rather a garden full of life, from the soil teeming with microorganisms to the air humming with insects and birds.

Here we are in the library at Wardington working on garden plans. We chose The Land Gardeners as our name – reflecting our respect for, and desire to be, good gardeners, and our passion for the land and soil. Drawn to the 1930s, we were inspired by the life and work of Beatrix Havergal who, with Avice Saunders, founded Waterperry School of Horticulture for Women in 1932 in Oxfordshire, and by the army of women who worked the fields during World War I and II as Land Girls.

We always strive to give a garden a purpose, particularly a productive purpose, as a place from which you can gather herbs, fruits, flowers and vegetables. We specialise in restoring walled gardens. Their high walls create perfect micro-climates to extend the growing season and to protect against animals such as deer and rabbits. But we don't want our gardens to take themselves too seriously and like a bit of playful exuberance. These are walled gardens and cutting gardens we have worked on in England, France, Italy and Zimbabwe.

It All Begins in the Soil

Soil is a delicate ecosystem made up of minerals, water, air, plant roots, organic matter, insects and a complex web of microorganisms. We rely on its health for our food and our future but, rather than treating it with care and respect, we continue to damage it at an alarming rate, behaving as if it were an inexhaustible resource. All our work at The Land Gardeners is guided by our shared belief in the importance of soil health.

Soil research has increasingly focused on the complex biological biome beneath the ground and the concept that soil is, in effect, the stomach of the plant. Astonishingly, there are more microorganisms in a teaspoon of soil than there are people in the world. These billions of microbes – about which we know so little – live symbiotically with plants, acting as their digestive system. The plants excrete carbon 'exudates' from their roots to feed the microorganisms, which in turn 'feed' the plant roots with minerals from the soil, thus releasing insoluble soil nutrients into plant-usable form. Nature is intricately balanced, and we now know that, just as caring for the gut flora within our intestines is vital to human health, so caring for the microbes in the soil is the essence of soil health. And if our soils thrive, our fruit and vegetables will take up more nutrients and we, in turn, will be healthier for eating them.

Supporting the soil is particularly important as we stand on the precipice of climate disaster. It is increasingly evident that we can use our soils to help cleanse the atmosphere, which faces dangerously high and rising levels of carbon dioxide. Unseen by the human eye, an awe-inspiring web of microbes can work with the soil, plants and air to 'sequester' carbon, thus allowing our soils to act as a carbon sink.

We have a long way to go. Globally, we have harmed our soils; years of ploughing and the indiscriminate use of pesticides and herbicides have taken their toll. Yet anyone who tends land – whether it's a square-metre garden or a farm spanning thousands of hectares – has the ability to nurture the soil and contribute to the health of our environment.

At The Land Gardeners, nurturing these soil microorganisms is at the forefront of our work, by growing organically and trialling new methods to feed them.

Partially digested compost after five weeks in our compost windrow.

Top from left to right
A winter workshop lunch at Wardington. Planting dahlias in mid-May. Naming roses for a rose workshop. Walled garden plans in the library. A tulip workshop with Charlie McCormick in Dorset.

Middle from left to right
A no-dig workshop with Charles Dowding at Wardington. Making compost windrows at our compost workshop. Polly Nicholson, one of our compost triallists, on an island off Mozambique. Dominic Amos, our Innovative Farmers researcher, and Emmanuel Taillard working on our programme of compost trials. Wildflower expert Charles Flower discussing the restoration of meadows. Compost windrows at our Farm Project.

Bottom from left to right
Results from our compost trials showing sweet peas grown in our compost developed longer stems and lasted for longer in the vase. A workshop lunch in the potting shed. Our design studio in London. Buckets of kale from our compost trials.

A Floral History

R̲ather like our business, the house and gardens at Wardington have developed in a haphazard way over time. Built in the fifteenth century as a nunnery, the house was reconfigured in 1665. In the early twentieth century it was again reworked, first by Clough Williams-Ellis, and later by G. H. Kitchin and Randall Wells – both advocates of the Arts and Crafts traditions of valuing craftsmanship over mass-manufacturing, and the romance of the medieval over the modern. The house now rambles over different levels, staircases appear from behind curtains and mullioned windows look out onto terraced lawns. The gardens weave around the house: a meander of outdoor 'rooms' backed by rust-coloured ironstone walls and high yew hedges. In summer it erupts in a profusion of wilful flowers, soaring up out of the beds and seeding in the walls and paths.

There is a playful inventiveness and a sense of unruly wildness about the house and gardens, and a similar spirit imbues our work. Outside, topiary creatures perched high above our heads watch as we bend and carry, dig and weed. Inside, whimsical, soft and buttery 1920s plasterwork exquisitely crafted by Molly Wells, Randall Wells' wife, lines the walls of the hall. Circus acts and acrobats tumble, balance and juggle around us as we carry flowers into the house, seemingly empathetic with our chores. Birds in icing-sugar plasterwork perch among zig-zag chevrons of ears of corn, and intricate patterns of fritillaries, primroses and violets remind us of the garden – all are still grown here today. Wardington is otherworldly: you will find large half-chewed dog bones on the rush matting in the hall; butterflies in the library, hiding from the cold; wisteria climbing in through the windows; and people endlessly appearing out of rooms.

However, perhaps what is most remarkable is that there has been a long tradition of growing flowers here, a tradition we have revived. When John Pease and his wife Dorothy Foster (later the first Lord and Lady Wardington) bought the house in 1917, the bones of the garden were already in place. Cath Congerton, who still lives in the village, spent twenty years as a gardener at Wardington Manor. Having gained her horticultural training as a Land Girl, she was hired soon after the Second World War, and remembers Lady Wardington as tireless in the garden and a passionate gardener. She recalls beehives nestled in the pergola border surrounded by a profusion of flowers, and rows of annuals in the cutting garden.

Lady Wardington particularly loved flowers, and during the 1940s, 50s and 60s, like other ladies of large country houses, she cut blooms from the borders and drove them down to eminent London florists Constance Spry and Pulbrook & Gould. It was a time when all florists sourced their flowers from English growers: narcissi and violets came by early train from Cornwall; lily of the valley travelled from Hampshire; and cars full of rambling roses, flowering blossom and herbaceous blooms came from country gardens and a wide variety of specialist growers.

Previous page The view from the cutting garden back towards the house in the early twentieth century.

Constance Spry – chosen florist of the Royal Family from the 1930s until her sudden death in 1960 – was hugely influential in this respect, incorporating flowers from hedgerows, vegetables and old roses into her innovative flower designs, including those for the wedding of the Duke and Duchess of Windsor in 1937 and the coronation of Queen Elizabeth II in 1953. She trained Rosamund Gould, who in 1956 partnered with Lady Pulbrook to found London florists Pulbrook & Gould, whose riotous, wild arrangements brimmed with flowers, foliage, berries and fruits from private English gardens.

When, in 1964, Audrey White married 'Bic' Pease, John and Dorothy's eldest son, she became the second Lady Wardington and years later continued her mother-in-law's tradition of growing flowers for cutting, filling her car with flowers and children. Lucy, her daughter, still recalls sharing many journeys to London surrounded by boxes of chrysanthemums, the smell of which gave her headaches. Audrey and Bic were avid gardeners and built up the garden over the years, meticulously recording in a notebook all the varieties they planted. However, in the late 1980s, Audrey gave up growing cut flowers, deciding her time was better spent elsewhere; she was far happier leaving flowers growing in the garden and buying lilies from Marks & Spencer for the house. The cutting gardens across the road were turned into allotments for the village and, years later, into pony paddocks for the children.

Then, in April 2004, while Audrey and Bic were on holiday, a fire broke out in the roof of Wardington Manor. Luckily, a passing postman saw the smoke and alerted their daughter Helen, who lived in part of the house. When the fire engines arrived, Helen realised that the water would destroy Bic's collection of rare atlases and bibles, so she rallied the village into action. Human chains were formed and they managed to save every last book and the majority of the furniture before the firefighters ordered everyone to leave as the fire romped through the floors.

After four years of painstakingly putting the listed building back together, and following the death of Bic, the second Lord Wardington, the family decided to sell in 2008. At the time, Bridget and her husband, Forbes, were living in New Zealand, and Forbes was desperate to return to England, but the children, who had spent three years running wild on the family farm, were reluctant to live in London again.

It is well known that one does not choose a house – a house chooses you! And in the case of Wardington Manor it chose the Elworthys, who moved there with their three small children in 2009.

The buttress borders are framed by scalloped yew hedging and backed by a wall covered in rampant roses. In the 1930s they gazed over a grass tennis court, now known as the top lawn. Both the yew hedging and roses remain today.

Top left Lady Pulbrook, photographed for *Vogue*.
Top right The Dorchester, decorated for a debutante ball with rhododendrons from Wardington.
Above left Dorothy, the first Lady Wardington.
Above right The 1961 wedding of the Duke and Duchess of Kent. Pulbrook & Gould used the beautiful white rose 'City of York' to decorate York Minster.
Right Constance Spry puts the finishing touches on an arrangement.

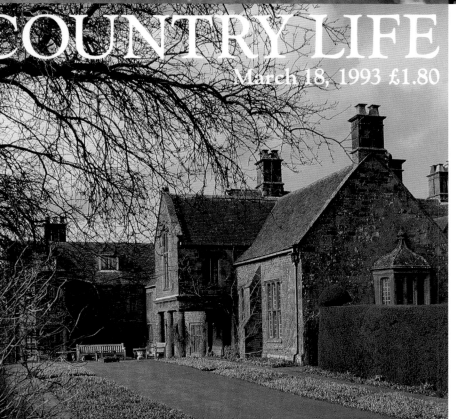

Top left Audrey, the second Lady Wardington, with Sir Malcolm Sargent and Sir Alec Guinness.

Top right Audrey (pictured with gardener Gordy Jones) overseeing the replanting of the pergola beds in 2010 from the comfort of an armchair on the top lawn.

Above left From left to right: Frank Lovell, 'Bic' (the second Lord Wardington), Cath Congerton (gardener for the first Lady Wardington), Audrey and Gordon Welbourne (the gardener in the 1980s).

Above right Audrey outside The Bishop's House in the village, where she lived in her later years.

Left Wardington Manor on the cover of *Country Life* in 1993.

Following page, left Flowers at the Ritz by Pulbrook & Gould, with roses from the garden at Wardington, for the wedding of Lady Pulbrook's granddaughter in June 1971. All the flowers were white, with the exception of two pyramids of pale pink peonies on the buffet.

Following page, right Flowers for the wedding of Lady Pamela Mountbatten and David Hicks in January 1960, by Pulbrook & Gould.

Creation of a Cutting Garden

For four years following the fire, the house lay empty but for teams of builders and joiners. There was this strange feeling of a broken house surrounded by immaculate gardens, which had been lovingly cared for by two gardeners: Philip Watts, who had been there for years, and Gordy Jones, whose first day had been the day of the fire. Only the beds closest to the manor were sacrificed to hold the tons of concrete needed to support the scaffolding. Despite this, the wonderful wisteria that clads the house survived unscathed. In late spring its gnarled branches still drip with lilac blooms, filling the house with their heavy, indolent fragrance. The wisteria, the magnificent old magnolia trees down the pond walk and the soaring hedges of yew are the real treasures of the garden.

Bridget had an over-riding sense that the garden at Wardington should not just be an expensive indulgence, but a working garden; so we decided to create our productive gardens at the manor. Having come from New Zealand, Forbes wanted to replace the many flower beds with sheep and trees. We had to convince him that our new business was going to pay its way and that, in time, the garden would become much more wild and natural.

The first year in any new garden is always one of discovery. In autumn the garden filled with pale-violet asters, soft Japanese anemones and swathes of bistort. Winter saw carpets of snowdrops and crocuses, clouds of blossom on the winter-flowering cherry, soft-petalled camellias and the shaggy blooms of witch hazel. Spring was ablaze with colour as the rhododendrons and azaleas along the pond walk came to life, garlands of wisteria engulfed the house, and wide beds of the palest iris marched away from the library door. It was only the walled garden and cut-flower beds that were no longer in use. The herbaceous borders were colourful but tired and in need of some love.

Guided by Audrey, Lady Wardington, who now lived in the village, we slowly learned about the garden, the traditions and routines of the way it was managed. How everything stopped at the beginning of the year to prune the hundred-year-old wisteria, how it took the gardeners six weeks to trim the old yew hedges and how the current head gardener's passion was growing dahlias – of which there were now few in the garden. Audrey's daily routine included walking from her cottage through the gardens, and in later years she sped around in her mobility scooter, often getting stuck down the pond walk. She was so encouraging. In the first year she was delighted to be involved in the replanting of the pergola borders, which had become overcrowded and weak. We pulled out comfy chairs from the library and, surrounded by gardening books and plans, Audrey sat and entertained us as we dug in perennials.

In an extraordinary coincidence during those early days of The Land Gardeners, eminent London florist Shane Connolly remarked that our flowers reminded him of those he had first come across in his early days as a young florist at Pulbrook & Gould, when ramshackle cars arrived – out of which elegant women dressed in tweed with cut glass accents would emerge with the most heavenly blooms. He had yearned to find the gardens that produced those flowers when he started out on his own, but Lady Pulbrook guarded them like a mother hen. It was such a sweet moment the day he came to pick up flowers from us and recognised Audrey sitting in the garden, shortly before she died in 2014. Once again Wardington was producing flowers for London's leading florists.

The view from the cutting garden, brimming with cosmos 'Dazzler', looking back towards the potting shed and glasshouse in the walled garden.

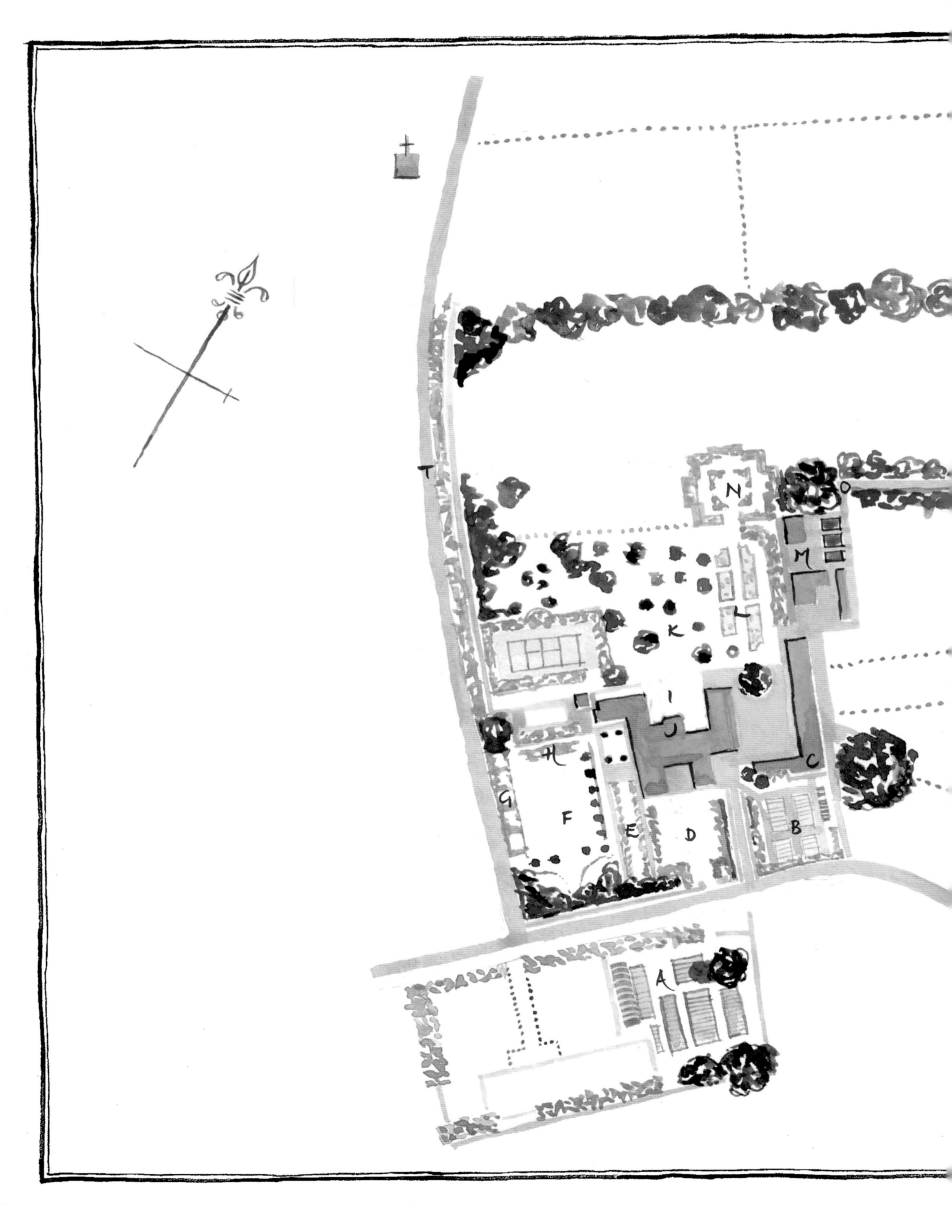

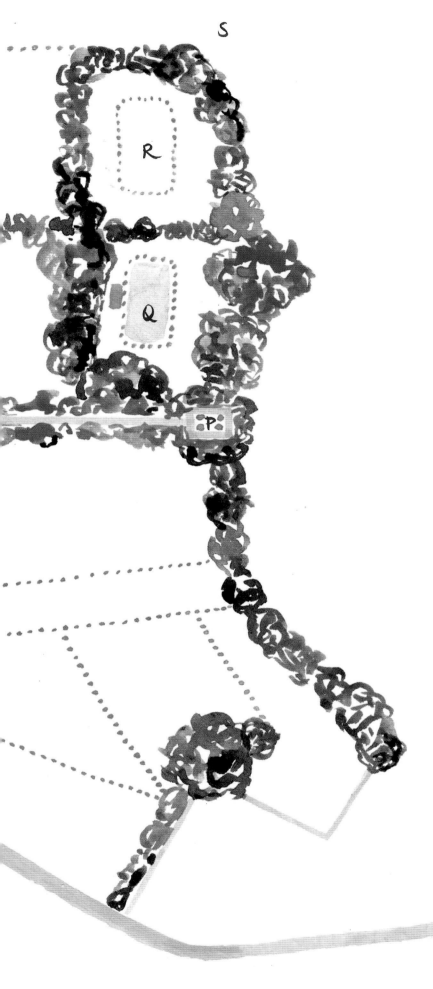

A The Cutting Garden
B The Walled Garden
C The Potting Shed
D The Bottom Lawn Borders
E The Iris Beds
F The Top Lawn
G The Butters Beds
H The Pergola Beds
I The Herb Garden
J The Flower Room
K The Orchard
L The Dahlia and Tulip Borders
M The Compost
N The Top of the Pond Walk
O The Pond Walk
P The Prison
Q The Nun's Bathing Pool
R The Bog Garden
S The Footpath to Fox Hill
T The Church Walk

The Gardens at
Wardington Manor

The Walled Garden

Over the years the walled garden at Wardington had gone the way of many walled gardens: home to a few rows of heeled-in perennials and a small compost area. When Bridget moved in, she reinstated the paths and the quadrant of four large central beds from the original plans for the garden. These are now predominantly rotated with a mix of cut flowers and annual vegetables. We find that the more we can mix flowers, herbs and vegetables, the happier they all are. Luckily, the soil in the walled garden is wonderful – deep and friable – and we take a minimal no-dig approach. Unless the soil has become badly compacted, we have found that just broad-forking in some compost in strips aerates the soil without exposing the light-sensitive microorganisms to too much sun, leaving narrow walkways for us to walk between the lines of plants.

We replanted the beds around the outside walls with a mix of perennials, including summer fruit (gooseberries, blackcurrants, blackberries, red and white currants – and rhubarb, which we also force under terracotta forcing pots), globe and Jerusalem artichokes, horseradish and herbs. We have an area for madder and woad, plants traditionally used for dyeing textiles. We planted heritage damsons, quinces and step-over apple trees – and we paid homage to the peach house, now sadly gone, by planting a young espaliered peach tree. We pruned an old fig that had grown unruly and unproductive; we dug around its base about 50 centimetres (20 inches) from the trunk, built a brick wall beneath soil level to restrict its roots, and ever since it has produced the most delicious figs.

We planted peonies that came all the way from Craigmore, the Elworthy family farm in New Zealand, which had been established in the 1980s by Bridget's mother-in-law, Fiona. In 2003, Bridget and Forbes had escaped the confines of London and were spending two years in the French countryside. Fiona went to visit them in the hottest summer in 500 years, arriving with a large leather trunk of peony roots that had travelled halfway around the world. Having been shocked into dormancy in the freezer before their journey, the roots were quickly planted into the garden in the ferocious heat, with little hope that they would survive. Astonishingly, some of them flowered in early autumn, in tune with the New Zealand seasons, and then again the following summer. Nine years later, we lifted some of them and brought them to Wardington. They are now planted in the perennial borders in the walled garden, interplanted with foxgloves in spring, and fennel later in the summer.

Rows of tulips march through the borders in spring, and alternating sweet peas and the 'Sunset' heritage runner bean, with its lovely pale-peach flowers, climb over a central arch. Teepees of sweet peas rotate around the beds following the brassicas, and in autumn cosmos 'Dazzler' and large dahlias like 'Elma E' and 'Otto's Thrill' abound among the many rows of vegetables.

In the north corner there is an old fruit room and potting shed with a fireplace in it, left over from its days as a school room for local children in the early 1900s. House particulars of 1917 talk of 'a good range of glass', including a 'Rose House, Two double-span Plant Houses, Double-span Carnation House, small Orchid House and heated pits'. Sadly, little of these remain today. The glasshouse we inherited is rather utilitarian, with missing panels of glass, but we still use it and have actually grown rather fond of it.

We often pick foliage from the walled garden, letting parsnips go to seed for their tall, lime-green umbelliferous flowers, collecting fragrant trugs of mint, rosemary and feather fronds of dill, fennel and asparagus. No plant is safe from our clutches; we even cut long canes of flowering raspberries for arrangements in autumn.

Purple and white foxgloves (*Digitalis purpurea* and *Digitalis purpurea* f. *albiflora*) and Sicilian honey garlic (*Nectaroscordum siculum*) in the walled garden in late spring. Rows of forced rhubarb tuck up beneath a quince (*Cydonia oblonga*).

Following page Gathering cosmos and dahlias from the walled garden in autumn. It is such an abundant time of the year – we are always astonished that the garden is still giving after a long summer.

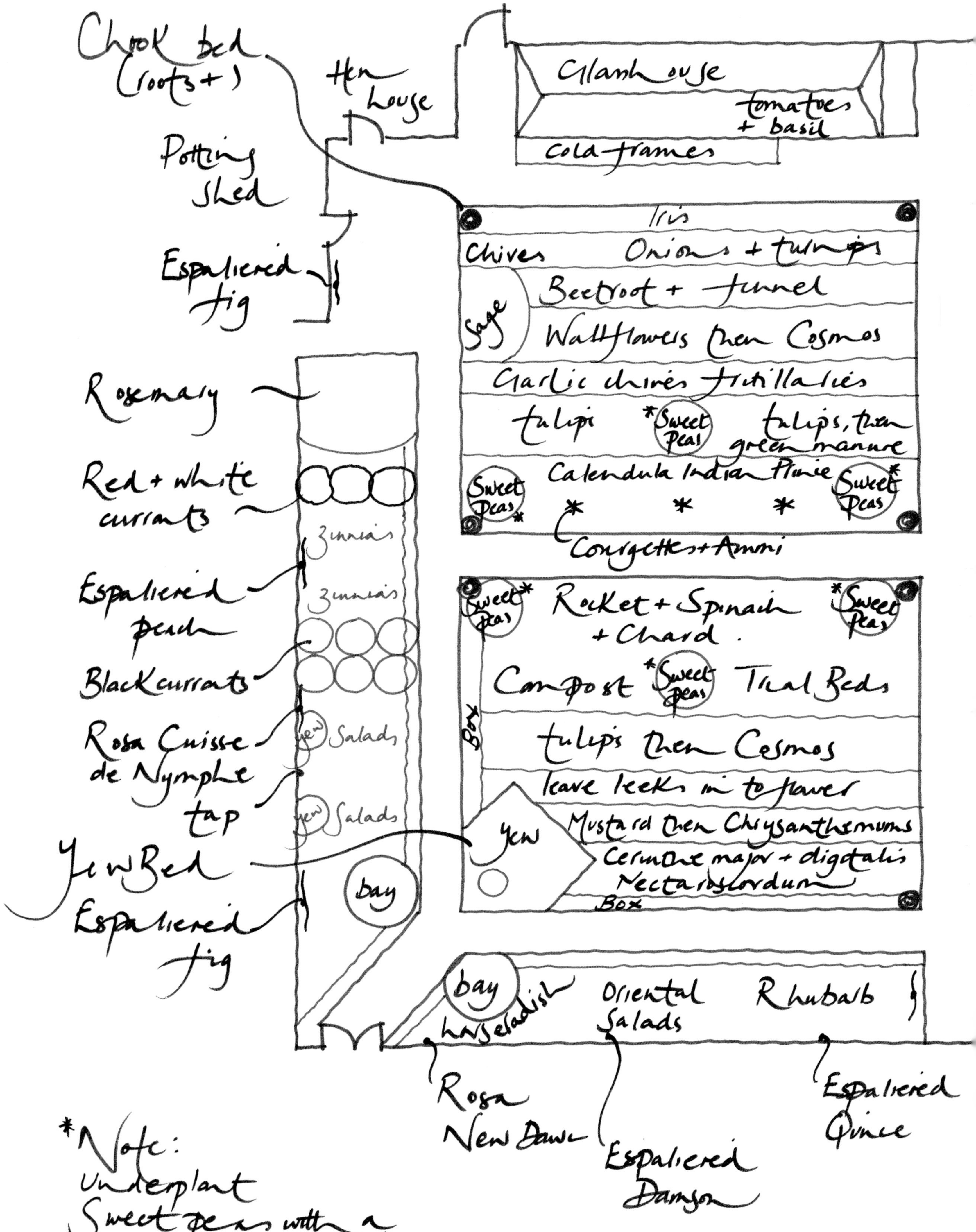

Chook bed
(roots +)

Hen House

Glasshouse

tomatoes
+ basil

cold frames

Potting Shed

Espaliered fig

Iris

Chives   Onions + turnips

Sage   Beetroot + fennel

Wallflowers then Cosmos

Garlic chives Fritillaries

Rosemary

tulips   *Sweet Peas   tulips, then green manure

Red + white currants

Sweet Peas *   Calendula Indian Prince   *Sweet Peas *

Zinnias

Courgettes + Ammi

Zinnias

Espaliered peach

Sweet Peas *   Rocket + Spinach + Chard.   *Sweet Peas

Blackcurrants

Compost *Sweet peas   Trial Beds

Yew Salads

Rosa Cuisse de Nymphe tap

tulips then Cosmos

Box

leave leeks in to flower

Yew Salads

Mustard then Chrysanthemums

Yew Bed

Yew   Cerinthe major + digitalis

Nectaroscordum

bay

Box

Espaliered fig

bay   Horseradish   Oriental Salads   Rhubarb

Rosa New Dawn

Espaliered Damson

Espaliered Quince

*Note:
Underplant
Sweet peas with a
circle of crimson clover
when seedlings are knee high

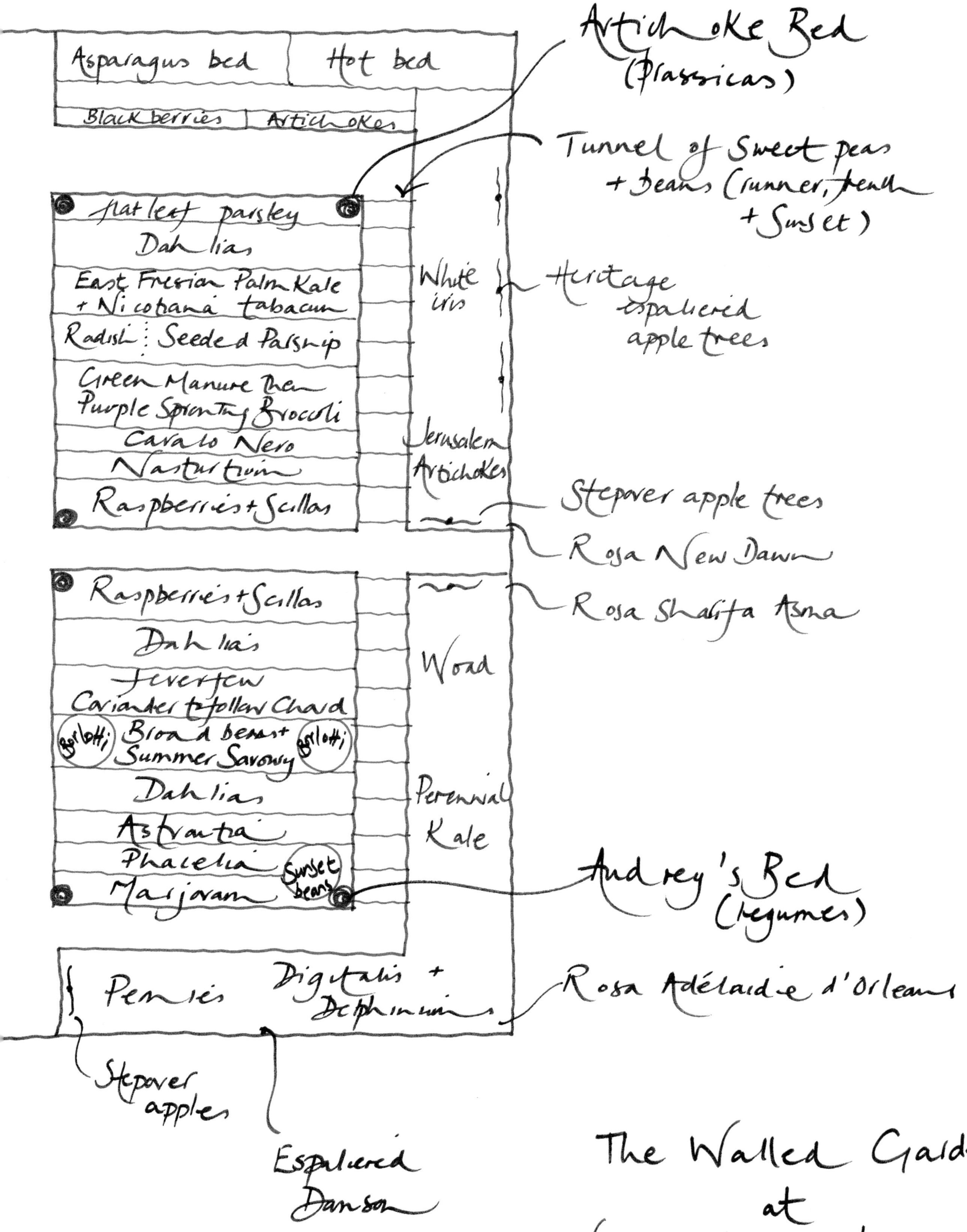

The Walled Garden at Waddington Manor

Plan labels:

- Asparagus bed | Hot bed
- Black berries | Artichokes
- flat leaf parsley
- Dahlias
- East Fresian Palm Kale + Nicotiana tabacum
- Radish : Seeded Parsnip
- Green Manure then Purple Sprouting Broccoli
- Cavalo Nero
- Nasturtium
- Raspberries + Scillas
- White iris
- Jerusalem Artichokes
- Raspberries + Scillas
- Dahlias
- Feverfew
- Coriander to follow Chard
- Borlotti | Broad beans + Summer Savoury | Borlotti
- Dahlias
- Astrantia
- Phacelia
- Marjoram | Sunset beans
- Woad
- Perennial Kale
- Pansies
- Digitalis + Delphiniums
- Stepover apples
- Espaliered Damson

Right-hand labels:
- Artichoke Bed (Brassicas)
- Tunnel of Sweet peas + beans (runner, french + Sunset)
- Heritage espaliered apple trees
- Stepover apple trees
- Rosa New Dawn
- Rosa Shalifa Asma
- Audrey's Bed (legumes)
- Rosa Adélaide d'Orléans

The Cutting Garden

Wrought-iron gates lead from the lower lawn across the road into the cutting garden. Originally used to grow cut flowers by the first Lady Wardington and later as allotments, it had long been turfed over and used as a pony paddock. Two old pear trees were all that remained of its earlier life. One spring, we were putting in a trough for the ponies when we discovered delicious dark topsoil, some 60 centimetres (2 feet) deep, no doubt built up over years of good cultivation. It was like finding treasure. Topsoil like this is so rare that we simply had to grow there. In fact, it only confirmed our belief that old walled gardens should, where possible, be used for growing plants. Their long cultivation means their soil is often healthy and rich – and would be far better used productively than as tennis courts or swimming pools. If only precious soil in walled gardens could be protected in the same way as precious houses.

The old cutting gardens thus became the ideal place for our ever-increasing collection of flowers. They are surrounded by low stone walls, from which we gather ivy for trails of greenery in winter, and a crimson hawthorn hedge on one side, whose pink blossoms last well in a vase.

We started with four large beds of roses: predominantly English shrub roses and hybrid teas. We love English shrub roses for their prolific flowering and loose, generous blooms, and hybrid teas for their vivacious colours and their large heads that soften as they open.

We planted perennials which, along with our roses, are the backbone of the cutting garden – euphorbias (*Euphorbia characias* subsp. *wulfenii*), purple toadflax (*Linaria purpurea* 'Canon Went'), phlox (*Phlox paniculata* 'Franz Schubert' and 'Diane'), goat's rue (*Galega officinalis*), delphiniums, peonies, scabious (*Scabiosa caucasica* 'Fama' and 'White'), eucalyptus (*Eucalyptus gunnii*), cardoons (*Cynara cardunculus*) and sedums (*Hylotelephium spectabile*).

And each year, we weave in our annuals. The brilliance of these is that every year we can change varieties, keeping our old favourites but also adding new ones: pink and white cosmos, bishop's flower (*Ammi majus*), bishop's weed (*Ammi visnaga*), Iceland poppies (*Papaver nudicaule* 'Champagne Bubbles') and white laceflower (*Orlaya grandiflora*). We have found that the latter fares better from its own seedlings than any we raise in the glasshouse, so we leave it happily growing in its own spot.

Our biennial foxgloves (*Digitalis purpurea*) and sweet rocket (*Hesperis matronalis* and *Hesperis matronalis* var. *albiflora*) are particularly good in early summer, and towering hollyhocks (*Alcea rosea*) come into their own in high summer. And we have invested in a polytunnel to extend the growing season for our tulips, love-in-a-mist (*Nigella damascena*), ranunculus, sweet peas and early-flowering anemones into late spring, when the garden is not yet into its stride. The polytunnel is often too hot in high summer but wonderful in late summer for delphiniums to protect their flowers from summer rain and to extend the season of dahlias and cosmos.

Here pale-pink spires of toadflax (*Linaria purpurea* 'Canon Went') are planted beneath the cutting garden walls.

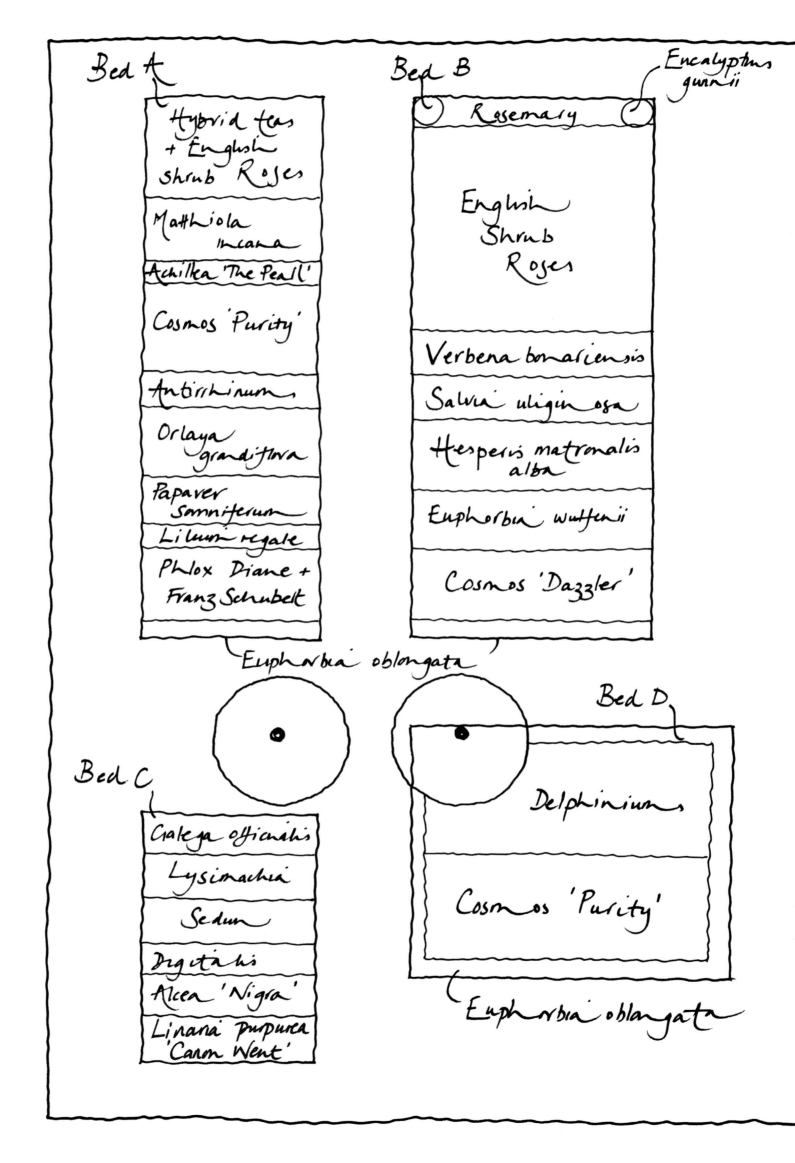

Bed A

Hybrid teas + English shrub Roses

Matthiola incana

Achillea 'The Pearl'

Cosmos 'Purity'

Antirrhinum

Orlaya grandiflora

Papaver Somniferum

Lilium regale

Phlox Diane + Franz Schubert

Bed B

Eucalyptus gunnii

Rosemary

English Shrub Roses

Verbena bonariensis

Salvia uliginosa

Hesperis matronalis alba

Euphorbia wulfenii

Cosmos 'Dazzler'

Euphorbia oblongata

Bed C

Galega officinalis

Lysimachia

Sedum

Digitalis

Alcea 'Nigra'

Linaria purpurea 'Canon Went'

Bed D

Delphinium

Cosmos 'Purity'

Euphorbia oblongata

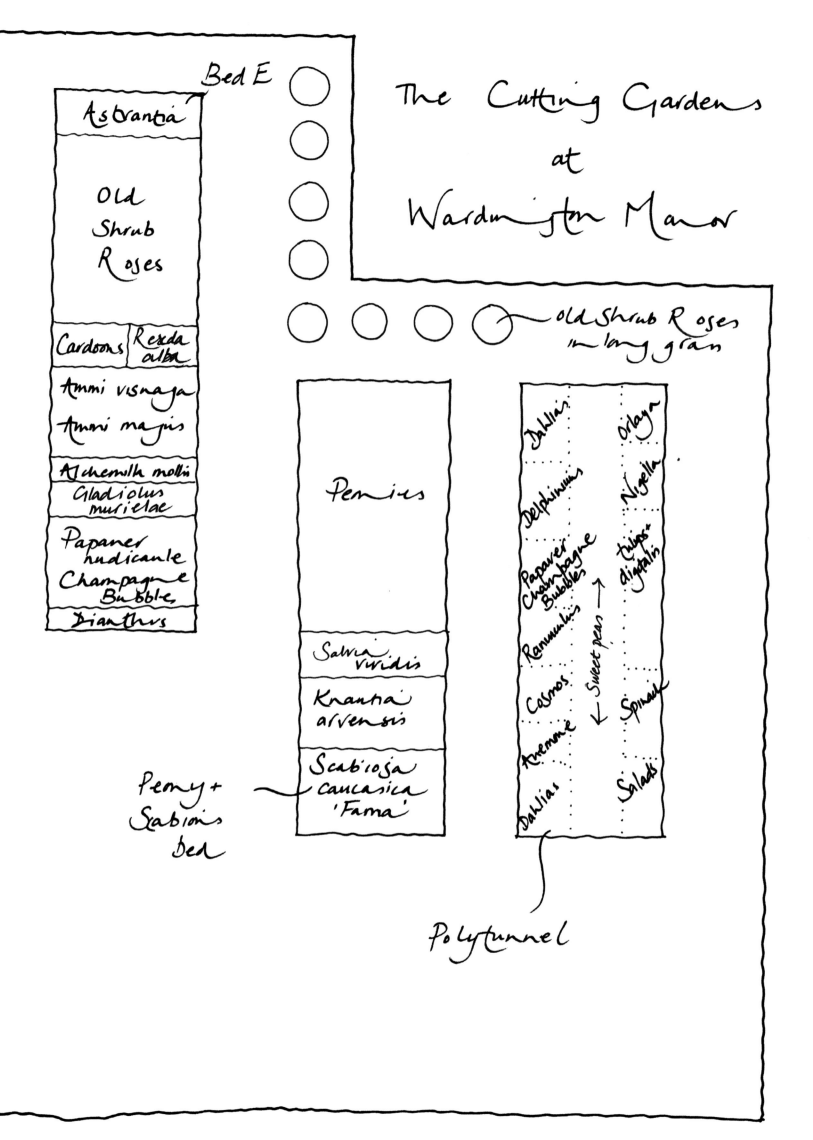

Bed E

The Cutting Gardens
at
Wardington Manor

Astrantia

Old
Shrub
Roses

Cardoons | Reseda
alba

Ammi visnaga

Ammi majus

Alchemilla mollis

Gladiolus
murielae

Papaver
nudicaule
Champagne
Bubble

Dianthus

Peonies

old Shrub Roses
in long grass

Salvia
viridis

Knautia
arvensis

Peony +
Scabious
Bed

Scabiosa
caucasica
'Fama'

Dahlias

Delphiniums

Papaver
Champagne
Bubbles

Ranunculus

Cosmos

Anemone

Dahlias

Origano

Nigella

tulips
digitalis

← Sweet peas →

Spinach

Salads

Polytunnel

The Dahlia and Tulip Borders

Gripped by an ever-increasing passion for tulips and dahlias, we realised that they would make the perfect plant partners: just as the tulips are over in late spring, the dahlias are ready to be planted; and once the dahlias have been dug up following the first frost of autumn, the tulips can be planted. So we decided we needed yet more cutting borders: dahlia and tulip borders. Our collection and the demand for them was expanding so fast that they were worthy of their own new dedicated area within the garden.

The area of orchard between the top of the pond walk and the house seemed like an ideal spot. The Edwardian topiary 'room' at the top of the walk had always felt somewhat disconnected from the yew 'rooms' that surrounded the house. New borders edged in yew would link the two areas and give us plenty of space to indulge our whims.

We planted our burgeoning collection of dahlias in late spring, after the last frost. Within a month the ground was covered, so there was no need to weed, and by the end of summer we had beds of blowsy dahlias – an instant garden. When the frost came and the dahlias went black, we lifted them and stored them in the potting shed for winter, and then in went the lines of tulips, along with some well-rotted compost. By the time the tulips had come up the following spring, they were so densely planted there was little room for weeds. Once the tulips and the frosts were over, we began the whole process again. If you want an easy year-round rotation for a flower bed, it is this.

Our first spring in the dahlia and tulip borders: 10,000 colourful tulips, tightly planted in rows in late autumn, bursting into bloom.

Top from left to right
The orchard before we cut our new 50-metre beds. Using a turf cutter is an easy, chemical-free technique that removes weed seed from the top layer and leaves you with a pile of turf that can be added to your compost. Our initial sketch for the new borders on the back of an envelope.

Bottom from left to right
We planted our dahlias in late spring, and by late summer they were as tall as us. Dahlias stored in crates of straw for the winter in the old potting shed. We gather tulips up to 1 metre (3 feet) long in spring by pulling rather than cutting.

The Perennial Borders

When we arrived at Wardington, the hundred-year-old perennial borders were immaculate 1970s style, all bright pink phlox and yellow goldenrod. Like all borders, they needed lifting and dividing, so we set about replanting them.

First we tackled the top lawn borders. The buttress beds were punctuated by tangled masses of variegated ivy, and edged with rows of vibrant orange 'Alexander' hybrid tea roses. We pulled them all out and quietened the borders with common valerian (*Valeriana officinalis*), sweet rocket (*Hesperis matronalis* var. *albiflora*), lady's mantle (*Alchemilla mollis*) and astrantia (*Astrantia major*). We moved some of the roses to the cutting garden – but now regret not keeping more, as they have become one of our favourites, adding fun to bowls of roses. Next, the pergola beds. Out with all the potentillas, hebes and orange Chinese lanterns, and in with the old roses and delphiniums.

The bottom lawn borders, framed with beautiful star magnolia (*Magnolia stellata*), now provide us with armfuls of cut flowers throughout the year. We start in spring, picking boughs of magnolia, green bracts of euphorbia (*Euphorbia characias* subsp. *wulfenii*), deep-red hellebores (*Helleborus* x *hybridus* 'Harvington Red') and the lime-green, early spring bells of fringe cups (*Tellima grandiflora*), followed by foxgloves (*Digitalis purpurea*), peonies, catmint (*Nepeta* 'Six Hills Giant') and giant scabious (*Cephalaria gigantea*), a lofty, light-yellow form that's wonderful for large, loose arrangements. In the height of summer we pick towards the back of the beds: tall spires of Culver's root (*Veronicastrum virginicum* 'Fascination'), clouds of meadow rue (*Thalictrum rochebruneanum*) and deep crimson eupatorium (*Eupatorium purpureum*). We leave the brown seed heads standing over the autumn, for the wildlife, cutting them down in early spring.

Then there are the iris beds. We pick iris (*Iris pallida* subsp. *pallida*) flowers for their intoxicating scent – heady, heavy and sweet – seizing our moment when we first see colour in their buds. These are underplanted with scillas (*Scilla siberica*), their blue blooms perfect for little bedside vases.

Common valerian self-seeds wildly around the herb garden. If it doesn't make its way into our biodynamic potions, the plumes of airy, vanilla-scented white flowers end up in a vase. White buddleja (*Buddleja davidii* 'White Profusion') keeps the butterflies happy, and hydrangea 'Annabelle' (*Hydrangea arborescens* 'Annabelle') is a useful source of fresh green in the autumn.

Flowering star magnolia (*Magnolia stellata*) in blossom in the bottom lawn borders. In spring we pick the emerging grey leaves of cardoons (*Cynara cardunculus*), fresh lime-green bracts of euphorbia (*Euphorbia characias* subsp. *wulfenii*) and purple honesty (*Lunaria annua*).

Following page Foxgloves (*Digitalis purpurea*), Turkish sage (*Phlomis russeliana*) and clary sage (*Salvia sclarea* var. *turkestanica*) stand tall above their skirts of lilac catmint (*Nepeta* 'Six Hills Giant'). Giant scabious (*Cephalaria gigantea*) flutter among delphiniums (*Delphinium* 'Blue Jade') at the back of the bottom lawn border. We love picking the floribunda rose 'Sally Holmes' for her trusses of creamy satin blooms and peach buds.

The Pond Walk

Walking down the pond walk is like falling down the rabbit hole in *Alice in Wonderland*. Planted in the Edwardian era, its spring-flowering trees and shrubs, now overgrown, tower over the path, some brazenly striving for attention with their hot colours, others pale and quietly alluring. Unlike in neighbouring gardens, acid-loving camellias, magnolias and rhododendrons grow well here, thanks to an unusual seam of acid soil running through the garden. In spring, we pick large branches of these glorious blooms, followed by delicate arching sprays of pearl bush (*Exochorda* x *macrantha* 'The Bride'), waxy blooms of eucryphia and then buckets of flowering lilac (*Syringa*), deutzia (*Deutzia* x *hybrida* 'Mont Rose'), beauty bush (*Kolkwitzia amabilis* 'Pink Cloud') and mock orange (*Philadelphus*).

At the bottom of the pond walk, Alice would land in a square room, referred to as a 'Quaint Sun Garden' in 1917, and now slightly unnervingly dubbed 'The Prison' because of its high walls. Tales abound of naked sun-bathing frolics down here in days gone by, but these days it is just us, rather tamely picking armfuls of martagon lilies (*Lilium martagon*), rambling roses and clematis in the summer.

The nun's bathing pool and charming old boathouse lie nearby, as if time has forgotten them. Even here we gather primulas (*Primula pulverulenta*) and hostas in spring from the banks of the stream, and hellebores (*Helleborus* x *hybridus*), foxgloves (*Digitalis purpurea*) and exquisite lily of the valley (*Convallaria majalis*) from the feet of the rhododendrons.

The Orchard

The wild and woolly orchard at Wardington shows that it is still possible to pick flowers from a garden without any borders at all. In spring we are often to be found up ladders, gathering large boughs of blossom from the fruit trees: serene, blush-white blossoms from the tall old Oxfordshire heritage apple trees, and the quince and pear trees; crazy, wonky Dr Seuss candy-floss-pink blooms from an old cherry tree; and, later in the summer, long boughs of the bright pink ruffs of a rampant rose that has scrambled impossibly high through the cherry tree's branches. An amelanchier (*Amelanchier lamarckii*) and a huge mock orange provide an understorey of blossom through into midsummer. And even in autumn, branches of small apples and quince give structure to large arrangements.

From the long grass in the orchard, we gather snowdrops (*Galanthus*), crocuses (*Crocus*), violets (*Viola odorata*), grape hyacinths (*Muscari*), primroses (*Primula vulgaris*), cowslips (*Primula veris*), camassias (*Camassia*), fritillaries (*Fritillaria persica*), 'Queen of the Night' tulips, clouds of cow parsley (*Anthriscus sylvestris*) and all types of narcissi – from the early-flowering 'Thalia' to the later-flowering pheasant's eye daffodil (*Narcissus poeticus* var. *recurvus*).

The Church Walk

Rarely visited during the busier months, the church walk sparkles in winter. It is an intimate little path, reminiscent of a Jane Austen novel, lined with thousands of bulbs (snowdrops, winter aconites, crocuses and cyclamens) and white lilac (*Syringa vulgaris* 'Madame Lemoine') in spring. In winter, we gather holly (*Ilex aquifolium*), for its berries and dark-green foliage.

Flamboyant powder-puff rhododendrons and azaleas brush against you as you descend the narrow path of the pond walk.

Topiary creatures stand guard at the top of the pond walk.
Opposite The orchard in spring comes alive with bulbs and blossoms.

The Flower Room

This is the Big Top of our floral circus: heaving with flowers, strewn with petals and leaves; gardeners stepping over puddles of spilled water, chilly fingers wet from washing flowers stems; large overflowing urns of rhododendrons sitting next to tiny silver cups of primroses. All of us breathe in the intoxicating scent of flowers, as if the air is thinner, lighter with the gentle fragrance of our blooms.

We are lucky to have a room that faces north and stays cool all year, but any corner of a house could work, ideally near a sink and tap, with a floor that can be easily cleaned, and shelves for storage. A spot in the kitchen or laundry, or a garden shed near an outside tap – either of these would be fine.

This is where we bring back our gathered flowers, leaving them to sit in buckets of water. It is where we prepare the flowers, conditioning and arranging them before we send them on their way. It is where we store vases, secateurs, gloves, floristry wire, waxed tape, luggage labels and buckets – all types of buckets, but our preference is for galvanised-steel or enamel, and the odd bucket with side handles is also useful. We have bundles of scrunched-up chicken wire and bowls of flower frogs or pinholders (vicious spiky things that you might find at the back of your granny's cupboard) that sit in the bottom of vases to hold flowers. They are essential and mean we don't use floral foam. This block of green foam once loved by florists is made of phenol formaldehyde, one of the oldest forms of plastic, and is not biodegradable. We also form wreaths of young branches and twigs in the bottom of vases as a natural way of holding flowers. It saves finding chicken wire and frogs in the compost.

Flamboyant dinner plate dahlias in the flower room: a riot of stripes ('Santa Claus'), hot pinks ('Otto's Thrill') and magenta ('Thomas Edison').

Tulips gathered in spring. We keep an old electric hob in the flower room to sear stems of flowers in boiling water – this helps them to last longer.
Opposite We propped up an old butler sink in the flower room – large enough to take huge tulip blooms.

Gathering

We gather at dawn and dusk. When the light is soft early in the morning or dimming as evening comes, this is the time to pick flowers. It is when there are low levels of transpiration, the plant cells are more turgid and stems less likely to flop. It is a rare time when we, like our plants and garden, are tranquil.

Quiet moments in the garden: no one around, a sense of calm. We can hear the birds, and we can see the shapes of shrubs and trees, sculpting them as we pick. This is perhaps our favourite part of growing flowers, looking carefully at our plants, choosing individual blooms to pick while knowing that we are helping the plant's growth, stimulating strong shoots and flowering.

Although we're convinced there's a secateur thief on the loose in the flower room as they never seem to be where we last put them, we try to use sharp secateurs to make clean cuts, as household scissors can crush the stems, preventing water uptake. Although tempted in the early days to carry armfuls of flowers back to the flower room, we now cut and immediately place them into buckets of water in the garden, choosing containers to suit the length of the stems, from tall buckets for cosmos to shallow old tin washing bowls for short-stemmed roses.

We wait until the flowers grown on single stems are fully open before gathering them (chrysanthemums, dahlias, zinnias). If picked too early, the buds will not open in a vase. For those plants with multiple buds on each stem, including both spires (agastache, delphiniums, snapdragons, larkspurs) and cluster flowers (ammi, phlox, lilacs and yarrow), we make sure they have at least one bud starting to open and one bud showing colour before cutting them.

Similarly, other flowers seem to settle into their own skin as they mature. Lilacs, hydrangeas and hellebores will drop when picked early in the season. However, wait until they are a little older and they are much more likely to last in a vase (hellebores in particular need to have developed their seed heads).

The flower room in spring, full of magnolia, cherry blossom and tulips. In the early morning and late afternoon, we gather armfuls of flowers, immediately placing them in water up to their necks.

Following page   Picking cosmos in the early days with Charlie McCormick as the sun rises in late autumn.

Setting off down the dahlia and tulip borders to gather buckets of dahlias for our London clients.
Opposite Enormous armfuls of cosmos. It is impossible to buy flowers like this in flower markets.

Preparing

This is busy, often very busy. Everyone in the team cutting and conditioning buckets of flowers, each variety like a different character in a play, all needing their hair preened and make-up done before they go on stage. Different varieties of flowers have their own individual whims. We are thankful for our undemanding stars: astrantia, whose light, airy flowers froth away, requiring no special attention; sedum, which just gets on with it; and the delightfully unneedy scabious and rosemary.

We start by cleaning the stems of any mud and cutting or pulling off any leaves that will be below the water line (to avoid them rotting). Resisting the urge to arrange them straight away, we place the flowers in buckets filled with water up to their necks. Flowers like to drink, to rest, as if settling themselves in the green room before a show. We give them a few hours in a cool, dark room, or even leave them overnight sometimes. This also allows any little bugs to crawl out. Peonies and hydrangeas are particularly fond of a long bath; they will be much perkier if you literally drown them in a bath of water overnight. All cut flowers prefer a vase of warm water, except for those grown from bulbs – for example tulips and hyacinths, which prefer cold water. We might add a dash of vinegar or lemon juice to keep the water acidic and thus less prone to bacteria. Some also say adding a spoonful of sugar helps feed them.

It's advisable to wear gloves when preparing flowers, taking particular care with euphorbias, the sap of which can burn the skin. For those flowers that are prone to wilt – such as hellebores, Iceland poppies, angelica, mock orange, lilacs, hydrangeas, euphorbias, dill, fennel, meadow rue and Japanese anemones – it's a good idea to recut the stems and instantly sear them, plunging the tips of the newly cut stems into a pan of boiling water. Over time, we have learned which flowers require searing, but we would advise: 'if in doubt, sear'. The length of searing time relates to the thickness of the stem: the fine stems of Iceland poppies or dill only need about 10 seconds, gradually increasing to, say, 20 seconds for the likes of euphorbias, hellebores and fennel, and the woodier stems of lilacs and hydrangeas need 30–40 seconds. As a general guide, watch to see when the air bubbles stop appearing from the base of the stems before removing them. It is particularly important to sear euphorbias as it prevents their milky sap from oozing into the water and blocking the vascular system of other flowers in the container. Sadly, searing is not effective in preventing seepage of sap from daffodils, so these do not make good friends in a vase with other flowers.

For plants with woody stems, such as lilac, hydrangea, mock orange and viburnum, we make a vertical cut up the base of the stem with secateurs; peeling the bark off the ends of the stems with a vegetable peeler can also help with the uptake of water. Lilac and mock orange flowers will last longer if the leaves are removed from their stems.

Our last tip is to keep experimenting. The manor house at Wardington can be chilly in the winter away from the fires and cool in the summer, so flowers generally last well. However, we will often pick a single bloom and leave it in a vase close to the Aga for a couple of days to see if it lasts. If it does, we know this variety will withstand the warmth of a client's showroom or centrally heated house.

We pull tulips, rather than picking them, effectively extending the length of their stems by about 20 centimetres (8 inches). We wash them thoroughly before they are placed in vases.

Potting Up

Potted flowering plants are a wonderful way of bringing some light and colour into the house during the cooler months of the year.

We start in the autumn, planting hyacinth, crocus, fritillary and grape hyacinth bulbs in tureens and old Constance Spry vases, and sitting paperwhite bulbs among pebbles, in water up to their middles, in containers ranging from silver jugs to large china bowls – the heady scent of their flowers will herald the first hint of spring.

Then, in winter, we bring winter-flowering bulbs into the house, inspired by the words of Vita Sackville-West: 'I somewhat nervously lifted a few clumps [of aconites] from the garden just as they were beginning to hump themselves in their round-shouldered way through the ground before the snow came, and transferred them with a fat ball of soil into a couple of low pans. They do not seem to have minded in the least, and are flowering like little suns, a gay sight on a winter morning.'

Following in her footsteps, we dig up clumps of snowdrops, winter aconites, hellebores and primulas, potting them in porcelain pots and silver cups to bring inside. Hellebores are particularly good at withstanding warmth and reduced light, and the distinctive almond scent of snowdrop 'Sam Arnott' fills the library. The moment they have bloomed, we put them back into the ground, tucking them up for another year.

As spring arrives, pots of the exquisite rhododendron 'Fragrantissimum' sit in the cool entrance hall, the fragrance of its delicate flowers permeating even the upper reaches of the house. These are followed by various scented-leaved pelargoniums and geraniums – rose, orange and mint – which come in from the glasshouse to adorn our tables with a profusion of foliage. As we pass, we take a leaf and gently rub it between our fingers: there is something deeply comforting about having a leaf of rose-scented geranium in one's pocket.

Then in high summer, royalty arrives as we bring in terracotta pots of tall, elegant regal lilies to grace the hall with their glamorous scent. They have sat outside all winter long, waiting for their moment to turn heads on a summer's evening.

To be honest, we are not the perfect candidates for pots as the pace of life is so busy that sometimes we forget to tend them! However, they soften a room and cheer the soul especially on cold, wet days when we are stuck inside.

In winter we force hyacinths (*Hyacinthus orientalis* 'White Pearl') in old tureens to welcome the first hint of spring.

Following page We also pot up snowdrops (*Galanthus nivalis*), primroses (*Primula vulgaris*) and Christmas roses (*Helleborus niger*) from the garden for bringing inside.

To Market

When we first started selling our flowers, we were intent on convincing people of the poetry of homegrown organic blooms: their sense of movement, their colours and scent, the natural, real beauty of a softly fading rose compared to its mass-market cousin. Most people don't realise that large-scale flower growers are heavy users of agricultural chemicals, relying in particular on preservatives to extend their longevity. Given a bunch of flowers, many people will instinctively breathe in their scent before placing them on the kitchen table, unaware of the potential effects of these chemicals on their health or the environment in which the flowers were grown, not to mention the carbon footprint of their journey.

Feeling our way into the business, we started supplying buckets of flowers to wholesale florists who shared our aesthetic. Soon we were gathering blooms small and tall for their creations, from tiny scillas to 3-metre (10-foot) boughs of old-fashioned rambling roses. We relished their requests for the unusual and the rare. When Shane Connolly asked us for gold flowers in high summer, we walked round and round the garden in a desperate quest for yellow and orange, only to realise we had golden buttercups growing in the field. These simple wildflowers were packed off to London and found themselves dancing down a palatial table in gold goblets at a state dinner, their petals glowing in the candlelight.

The following winter saw us answering Flora Starkey's call for dead and dying flowers – preferably with thorns – for the opening of 'Savage Beauty', the Alexander McQueen exhibition at the Victoria and Albert Museum in London. Luckily we hadn't yet cut down our borders that year, so we were able to gather buckets of seed heads and brambles. We remember stuffing boughs of thorny brambles into a local builder's van among his tools, as he looked on open-mouthed in astonishment.

Over time the novelty of driving to London each week, sometimes twice, wore thin, as did squeezing tall willowy stems into our old Land Rover without damaging them. Instead, we bought an old van and employed David, our driver, to deliver directly to private clients in London. We packed large wicker baskets with vases of flowers to fill their houses; at the same time, we started a scheme delivering fresh organic blooms in large zinc buckets to London doorsteps each week. And finally, in a weak moment, we took on arranging flowers for events – only to discover that we rather enjoyed the experience of creating a production. There was something of the travelling circus that appealed to our love of theatre.

To anyone starting out, we would stress that it is important to focus on your style and your story, as this will help define your business. Decide whether you want just to grow flowers or to arrange them as well, keeping in mind that arrangements can be a valuable source of income, particularly for large events or weddings. Consider whether you enjoy creating close relationships with a few clients or sending flowers by mail order to customers you never see. And like us, you may find that teaching and running workshops is an enjoyable and worthwhile addition to your business.

Circus-tent stripes and partying dahlias.

the land gardeners

delivery note

no: 1728

date :

The Land Gardeners' travelling
circus: our flowers at weddings
and events, and buckets waiting
to be delivered to London
doorsteps.

Previous page, left
A quiet moment in the
flower room.
Previous page, right
Dahlias under the Big Top.

Year of Flowers

Spring

The love of gardening is a seed that once sown never dies.

Gertrude Jekyll

To do

EARLY/MID-SPRING

Under cover

Start sowing hardy annuals and perennials under cover (i.e. in a glasshouse or on a windowsill).
From mid-spring, start sowing half-hardy annuals.
Prick out and pot up seedlings when ready.
Plant dahlia tubers in pots to gain a head start in the garden and for taking root cuttings.
Pot up cuttings of pelargoniums from last autumn.

In the garden

Prepare your soil by aerating it and mulching the beds with compost.
Hoe the garden on warm, sunny days to keep on top of weeds; continue throughout the growing season.
Sow green manures in areas of bare soil; continue throughout the year.
Keep tulips well-watered as they appear.
Plant autumn-flowering bulbs, such as Abyssinian gladiolus (*Gladiolus murielae*), in the garden or in pots.
Direct-sow hardy annuals; harden off and plant out hardy annual seedlings; continue through spring.
Plant new perennials; lift and divide late-summer-flowering perennials.
Finish planting bare-root roses, trees and shrubs.
Start making compost windrows; continue throughout growing season.
Feed seedlings with compost teas and liquid feeds; continue throughout growing season.
Treat dahlia and delphinium borders with nematodes every six weeks to protect against slugs.
Remove flower heads and prune mophead hydrangeas in mid-spring.

LATE SPRING

Under cover

Continue sowing half-hardy annuals under cover and pricking out and potting up seedlings.

In the garden

Continue preparing soil, hoeing and sowing green manures (see early/mid-spring).
Continue making compost and feeding seedlings (see early/mid-spring).
Lift tulips, unless you are leaving them in the ground.
Harden off and plant out half-hardy annuals and other frost-tender plants (e.g. cosmos) after the last frost.
Divide dahlia tubers that have been stored over winter and plant out in beds following the last frost; keep well-watered.
Treat dahlia and delphinium borders with nematodes six weeks after last treatment to maintain protection.
Start staking plants that need support, e.g. delphiniums, aconitums, thalictrum, peonies.

In spring we cut magnolia (*Magnolia* x *soulangeana*) to bring into the hall.

To gather

EARLY/MID-SPRING

Bulbs and corms

Anemone coronaria (anemone)

Crocus vernus (spring crocus)

Fritillaria imperialis (crown imperial fritillary)

Fritillaria meleagris (snake's head fritillary)

Fritillaria persica (Persian lily fritillary)

Hyacinthus orientalis (hyacinth)

Leucojum aestivum 'Gravetye Giant' (summer snowflake)

Leucojum vernum (spring snowflake)

Muscari (grape hyacinth)

Narcissus (daffodil), e.g. 'Jenny', 'Thalia', 'Actaea'

Scilla luciliae/*Chionodoxa luciliae* (glory of the snow)

Scilla siberica (scilla)

Tulipa (tulip), e.g. single earlies, double earlies,
    mid-seasons, Darwin hybrids, Triumphs, Viridiflora

Biennials

Erysimum (wallflower)

Lunaria annua (honesty – purple) and var. *albiflora* (white)

Myosotis sylvatica (forget-me-not)

Perennials

Bergenia (elephant's ear)

Helleborus argutifolius (Corsican hellebore)

Helleborus x *hybridus* (hybrid Lenten rose)

Primula vulgaris (primrose)

Trees and shrubs

Amelanchier lamarckii (juneberry)

Camellia (camellia)

Chaenomeles (Japanese quince)

Euphorbia characias subsp. *wulfenii* (Mediterranean spurge)

Magnolia x *soulangeana* (magnolia)

Magnolia stellata (star magnolia)

Prunus (cherry), e.g. 'Tai-haku' (great white cherry)

Prunus persica (peach)

LATE SPRING

Bulbs and corms

Allium (allium)

Camassia (camassia)

Convallaria majalis (lily of the valley)

Fritillaria imperialis (crown imperial fritillary)

Fritillaria meleagris (snake's head fritillary)

Fritillaria persica (Persian lily fritillary)

Gladiolus colvillei 'The Bride' (gladiolus)

Muscari (grape hyacinth)

Narcissus (daffodil), e.g. *Narcissus poeticus* var. *recurvus*
    (pheasant's eye daffodil)

Nectaroscordum siculum (Sicilian honey garlic)

Ranunculus (ranunculus)

Tulipa (tulip), e.g. single lates, double lates, multi-flowered,
    Darwin hybrids, parrot, Viridiflora

Hardy annuals

Cerinthe major 'Purpurascens' (honeywort)

Consolida ajacis (larkspur), e.g. 'White'

Echium vulgare (viper's bugloss), e.g. 'Blue Bedder'

Papaver nudicaule (Iceland poppy), e.g. 'Champagne
  Bubbles'

Papaver somniferum (opium poppy)

Reseda alba (white mignonette)

Biennials

Angelica archangelica (angelica)

Anthriscus sylvestris 'Ravenswing' (black cow parsley)

Digitalis purpurea (foxglove)

Hesperis matronalis (sweet rocket)

Hesperis matronalis var. *albiflora* (sweet rocket – white)

Matthiola incana (Brompton stock)

Matthiola incana 'Pillow Talk' (garden stock)

Myosotis sylvatica (forget-me-not)

Perennials

Anthriscus sylvestris (cow parsley)

Aquilegia (granny's bonnet)

Euphorbia oblongata (Balkan spurge)

Linaria purpurea (purple toadflax), e.g. 'Canon Went'

Polygonatum x *hybridum* (Solomon's seal)

Tellima grandiflora (fringe cup)

Trees and shrubs

Cydonia oblonga (quince)

Exochorda x *macrantha* 'The Bride' (pearl bush)

Kolkwitzia amabilis 'Pink Cloud' (beauty bush)

Magnolia x *soulangeana* (magnolia)

Malus x *domestica* (apple blossom)

Malus sylvestris (crab apple blossom), e.g. 'Evereste'

Rhododendron (rhododendron and azalea)

Syringa (lilac)

Viburnum opulus 'Roseum' (snowball tree)

Weigela

We are collaborating with Emmanuel Taillard on soil trials and a new cutting garden at Château de la Rongère, in the Pays de la Loire region of France.
Opposite A 1950s mural from a studio in a National Trust garden in Zimbabwe we were asked to restore. The house and gardens were built by Virginia and Stephen Courtauld, who had previously lived at Eltham Palace in London. In the early 1950s they escaped post-war England, flying over Africa in a Lancaster bomber in search of a place to settle. They found La Rochelle, a beautiful stretch of valley nestled in the verdant foothills near the Mozambique border.

Previous page, left The old wisteria survived works on the house following the fire in 2004. Its magnificent twisted limbs enfold the Jacobean walls.
Previous page, right In spring we gather daffodils, buttercups, cow parsley and apple blossom from the orchard – all easy to grow and to pick.

Striped tulips evoke seventeenth-century Dutch paintings. 'Helmar', 'Grand Perfection' and 'Raspberry Ripple' flirt with the dark-red 'Jan Reus', almost black 'Paul Scherer' and 'Black Charm', and a few parrot tulips – 'Apricot Parrot' and 'Flaming Parrot'.

Opposite Our tall tulips move and unfurl, dancing with the Grecian lady in the plasterwork that lines the walls of the hall. In a vase, these languid creatures bend and curve, their shot-silk petals opening wide, their colours intensifying as they age, beautiful even as they die.

Previous page, left The old boathouse hidden in a cloud of cow parsley by the nun's bathing pool in spring. We gather huge branches of lilac (*Syringa*), cherry blossom (*Prunus*) and dog roses (*Rosa canina*) from this wild part of the garden.

Previous page, right Jugs of labelled tulips ready for a spring workshop: 'Apricot Parrot' and 'Black Charm' with striped 'Raspberry Ripple' and 'Flaming Club'. The scent of rhododendron 'Fragrantissimum' floods the hall.

Cheery daffodils, tulips and camellias in vases: the creamy yellow trumpet of *Narcissus* 'Mount Hood' turns to pure white as it ages.
Opposite Starry juneberry (*Amelanchier lamarckii*) in the library in late spring.

Previous page Cow parsley (*Anthriscus sylvestris*) skirts an old heritage apple tree at the top of the pond walk – wonderful to pick in late spring.

Top left Delicate daffodils – narcissi 'Segovia', 'Thalia' and 'Silver Chimes' – in a shell vase.

Top right Waxy blooms on smooth branches of Japanese quince (*Chaenomeles*), with camellia 'Debbie', in early spring.

Above left Pink puffs of cherry blossom (*Prunus*) at Soane Britain.

Above right White and purple lilac (*Syringa vulgaris* 'Madame Lemoine' and 'Charles Joly') off to a late spring party.

Top left The huge iridescent goblets of the Darwin hybrid tulip 'Apricot Impression' – more poppy than tulip.

Top right Hanging bells of Sicilian honey garlic (*Nectaroscordum siculum*), fresh white sweet rocket (*Hesperis matronalis* var. *albiflora*) and early-flowering peony 'Gardenia' in the flower room.

Above left The striking petals of tulips 'Flaming Club' and 'Raspberry Ripple' reflex and contort as they fade.

Above right Pheasant's eye daffodils (*Narcissus poeticus* var. *recurvus*) in a tiny silver jug.

Summer

Summer afternoon, summer afternoon; to me those have always been the two most beautiful words in the English language.
Henry James

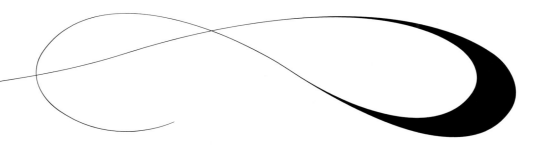

SINCE FOR REFRESHMENT
ONCE COMETH HENCE,
LET WIT CAST OFF THE
DEAR DULL YOKE OF SENSE

To do

EARLY SUMMER

Under cover

Take softwood cuttings of perennials.

In the garden

Continue hoeing on warm, sunny days to keep on top of weeds before they appear!
Continue sowing green manures in areas of bare soil.
Continue making compost windrows throughout the growing season.
Continue feeding seedlings and plants with compost teas and liquid feeds.
Direct-sow hardy annuals; harden off and plant out hardy and half-hardy annual seedlings.
Treat delphinium and dahlia beds with nematodes every six weeks to protect against slugs.
Stake, water and feed dahlias; continue throughout summer.

MID/LATE SUMMER

Under cover

Sow biennials.
Collect seed in late summer.
Take softwood cuttings of perennials in high summer; take pelargonium cuttings at the end of summer.
Order next year's spring and summer bulbs for the garden.
At the end of summer, order winter bulbs for forcing and potting inside.

In the garden

Continue preparing the soil, hoeing and sowing green manures (see early summer).
Continue making compost and feeding plants (see early summer).
Stake, water and feed cosmos; continue throughout summer.
Cut back perennials, e.g. catmint, in midsummer once they have finished flowering to encourage new growth.
Divide bearded irises every three to five years after flowering.
Feed roses after their first flush of flowering with compost; keep deadheading them.
Keep the garden well-watered.

Arts and Crafts plasterwork crafted by Molly Wells in the 1920s lines the walls. Serpents weave along the architrave through spring flowers grown in the garden, and a juggler on stilts keeps us merry. We try to live by the words of the quote above the doorway: 'Since for refreshment one cometh hence, let wit cast off the dear dull yoke of sense.' Irises and delphiniums relax in an ironstone jug, and Soane Britain's fabric 'Tendril Vine' climbs the four-poster bed.

To gather

Bulbs and corms

Allium (allium)

Camassia (camassia)

Galtonia candicans (summer hyacinth)

Gladiolus colvillei 'The Bride' (gladiolus)

Lilium martagon (martagon lily)

Lilium regale (regal lily)

Nectaroscordum siculum (Sicilian honey garlic)

Ornithogalum magnum 'Moskou' (star of Bethlehem)

Ornithogalum thyrsoides (chincherinchee)

Hardy annuals

Ammi majus (bishop's flower)

Ammi visnaga (bishop's weed)

Anethum graveolens (dill)

Bupleureum rotundifolium 'Griffithii' (hare's ear)

Calendula officinalis (pot marigold), e.g. 'Indian Prince'

Centaurea cyanus (cornflower)

Cerinthe major 'Purpurascens' (honeywort)

Consolida ajacis (larkspur), e.g. 'White'

Echium vulgare (viper's bugloss), e.g. 'Blue Bedder'

Euphorbia oblongata (Balkan spurge)

Lathyrus odoratus (sweet pea)

Nigella damascena (love-in-a-mist)

Orlaya grandiflora (white laceflower)

Papaver nudicaule (Iceland poppy), e.g. 'Champagne Bubbles'

Papaver somniferum (opium poppy)

Reseda alba (white mignonette)

Salvia viridis (clary sage)

Scabiosa atropurpurea (scabious)

Half-hardy annuals

Antirrhinum majus (snapdragon)

Cosmos bipinnatus (cosmos)

Didiscus coerulea (blue laceflower), e.g. 'Blue Lace'

Moluccella laevis (bells of Ireland)

Nicotiana alata (tobacco plant), e.g. 'Grandiflora'

Nicotiana sylvestris (tobacco plant)

Tropaeolum majus (nasturtium), e.g. 'Black Velvet'

Zinnia (zinnia)

Biennials

Anthriscus sylvestris 'Ravenswing' (black cow parsley)

Daucus carota (wild carrot)

Digitalis purpurea (foxglove)

Hesperis matronalis (sweet rocket – lavender)

Hesperis matronalis var. *albiflora* (sweet rocket – white)

Matthiola incana (Brompton stock)

Perennials

Achillea ptarmica 'The Pearl' (sneezewort)

Aconitum 'Stainless Steel' (monk's hood)

Agastache 'Blue Fortune' (giant hyssop)

Alcalthaea x *suffrutescens* 'Parkallee'
   (hollyhock/marshmallow cross)

Alchemilla mollis (lady's mantle)

Astrantia major (masterwort)

Campanula lactiflora (milky bellflower)

Centranthus lecoqii (valerian – mauve)

Centranthus ruber (valerian – red), and 'Albus' (white)

Cephalaria gigantea (giant scabious)

Cynara cardunculus (cardoon)

Delphinium elatum (delphinium)

Dianthus (carnation)

Foeniculum vulgare (fennel)

Iris (iris)

Knautia arvensis (field scabious)

Levisticum officinale (lovage)

Linaria purpurea (purple toadflax), e.g. 'Canon Went'

Nepeta (catmint), e.g. 'Six Hills Giant'

Origanum (marjoram)

Penstemon (beard tongue)

Peonia lactiflora (peony)

Persicaria bistorta (bistort), e.g. 'Superba'

Phlox paniculata (border phlox)

Salvia patens (gentian sage)

Scabiosa caucasica (Caucasian scabious), e.g. 'Fama'

Silene fibriata (fringed campion)

Thalictrum rochebruneanum (meadow rue)

Valeriana officinalis (common valerian)

Verbascum (mullein)

Verbena bonariensis (Argentinian vervain)

Veronicastrum virginicum (Culver's root)

Foliage (herbs, vegetables)

Mentha spicata (mint)

Pastinaca sativa (parsnip)

Petroselinum hortense 'Gigante di Napoli' (flat-leaved
   parsley)

Rosmarinus officinalis (rosemary)

Rubus idaeus 'Autumn Bliss' (raspberry)

Climbers

Clematis (clematis), e.g. 'Prince Charles'

Hydrangea anomala subsp. *petiolaris* (climbing hydrangea)

Lonicera periclymenum (honeysuckle), e.g. 'Serotina'

Rosa (rose)

Trees and shrubs

Buddleja (butterfly bush)

Deutzia x *hybrida* (deutzia), e.g. 'Mont Rose'

Hydrangea arborescens 'Annabelle' (sevenbark)

Hydrangea macrophylla (mophead hydrangea)

Hydrangea quercifolia (oak-leaved hydrangea)

Kolkwitzia amabilis 'Pink Cloud' (beauty bush)

Philadelphus (mock orange)

Rosa (rose)

Spiraea nipponica (spirea), e.g. 'Snowmound'

Syringa (lilac), e.g. 'Katherine Havemeyer'

Viburnum opulus 'Roseum' (snowball tree)

Weigela

Peonies on the windowsill at the Elworthy peony farm, Craigmore, in New Zealand: 'Gardenia', 'Chippewa' and 'Illini Warrior' in a silver cup. We are looking into plant partnering peonies with herbs and producing organic peony root for medicinal use.
Opposite Peony 'Karl Rosenfield' is one of many that have come from Craigmore in New Zealand. Crimson double flowers are carried on strong stems on this mid-season peony.

Previous page Fragrant, deep-pink English shrub rose 'Royal Jubilee' flowers throughout summer.
Pages 120–121 Rose blooms in tiny jugs, individually labelled for teaching a workshop.

An early Dutch honeysuckle (*Lonicera periclymenum* 'Belgica') winds its way over the gate at the top of the steps leading down to the bottom lawn.
Opposite   A pale-pink climbing rose, planted long before we arrived at Wardington, smothers the tack room beside the herb garden.

Previous page   The bottom lawn border in early summer: deep-purple iris 'Black Swan' among the pale pinks, peaches and lilacs of valerian (*Centranthus ruber* and *Centranthus lecoqii*), foxgloves (*Digitalis purpurea*) and the nodding heads of geranium 'Walküre'.

Following page   When we arrived at Wardington, we replanted the entire length of the Edwardian pergola beds with blue delphiniums, rising up among old shrub roses 'Cardinal Richelieu' and 'Comte de Chambord'.

We gather pale-yellow giant scabious (*Cephalaria gigantea*) and steely-blue monk's hood (*Aconitum* 'Stainless Steel') from the back of the borders.
Opposite   Two hybrid tea roses, pale pink 'Aphrodite' and salmon-pink 'Blessings', share a bowl with soft vanilla-yellow 'Jude the Obscure'.
The sweet peas 'Mollie Rilstone' and 'Prince Edward of York' and Iceland poppies (*Papaver nudicaule* 'Champagne Bubbles') float like butterflies.

Following page   We found the hybrid tea vermilion 'Alexander' rose growing in the garden when we arrived. We now mix it with pale-pink English
shrub roses like 'Geoff Hamilton' and 'The Shepherdess' for its vibrant colour.

Top left We bring many varieties of pelargonium inside all summer long.

Top right Dark, almost black hollyhocks (*Alcea rosea* 'Nigra') in our flower room – a bit temperamental as cut flowers, they are glorious when they decide to cooperate, twisting and turning in the vase.

Above left Glamorous regal lilies (*Lilium regale*) exude their heavenly scent in the early evening.

Above right Carnations (*Dianthus caryophyllus*) make lovely bedside posies.

Top left Pastel-hued foxgloves (*Digitalis purpurea* 'Sutton's Apricot').

Top right A huge urn of feathered goat's rue (*Galega officinalis*) and umbellifers, fennel (*Foeniculum vulgare*) and bishop's weed (*Ammi visnaga*), in the library.

Above left A bowl of peonies and roses. Peony 'White Wings' nestles among roses 'Gentle Hermione', 'Gertrude Jekyll' and the pale-apricot climber 'Crepuscule'.

Above right We pick milky bellflowers (*Campanula lactiflora* 'Prichard's Variety') for their haze of blue.

Autumn

Autumn in felted slipper shuffles on, muted yet fiery.
Vita Sackville-West

To do

EARLY AUTUMN

Under cover

Continue collecting seed.
Sow hardy annuals for next year, if you want to get a head start.
Plant ranunculus and anemones under cover for early spring flowers, or over-winter them inside in pots.
Plant hardy annuals, e.g. love-in-a-mist (*Nigella damascena*), white laceflower (*Orlaya grandiflora*) and Iceland poppies (*Papaver nudicaule*), under cover for early spring flowers.

In the garden

Continue hoeing the garden on warm, sunny days to keep on top of weeds before they appear!
Sow the last of your green manures in areas of bare soil to keep covered over winter.
Continue making compost windrows throughout the growing season.
Continue feeding seedlings and plants with compost teas and liquid feeds.
Plant out biennial seedlings and perennial seedlings from seeds sown early in the summer.
Mulch peonies with compost.
Water and feed dahlias.
Plant spring-flowering bulbs (e.g. daffodils, crocuses, fritillaries and hyacinths) and hardy summer-flowering bulbs (e.g. alliums, lilies).
Prune lacecap hydrangeas after flowering, to prevent seed developing.

MID/LATE AUTUMN

Under cover

Take root cuttings from perennials.
Force hyacinth bulbs and pot up crocuses.
Pot up paperwhite bulbs, or sit them among pebbles in shallow water, repeating every few weeks for a succession of flowers throughout winter.

In the garden

Give beds a light covering of compost.
Finish making compost windrows and cover them for winter.
Plant tulips in pots and the garden in late autumn.
Lift and divide early-spring-flowering perennials.
Cut back peony foliage, when brown, to 10 centimetres (4 inches) above soil level.
Plant bare-root roses; lightly prune roses to stop windrock.
Remove dahlia tubers from the ground after the first frosts; wash and store.
Plant evergreen shrubs and trees.

An explosion of pink – dahlias 'Elma E' and 'Gerrie Hoek' – and orange dahlia 'Eileen' in a Constance Spry vase.

To gather

Bulbs and corms

Colchicum autumnale (autumn crocus)

Cyclamen hederifolium (cyclamen)

Gladiolus murielae (Abyssinian gladiolus)

Nerine bowdenii (Bowden Cornish lily)

Hardy annuals

Ammi majus (bishop's flower)

Ammi visnaga (bishop's weed)

Anethum graveolens (dill)

Bupleureum rotundifolium 'Griffithii' (hare's ear)

Echium vulgare (viper's bugloss), e.g. 'Blue Bedder'

Euphorbia oblongata (Balkan spurge)

Reseda alba (white mignonette)

Salvia viridis (clary sage)

Half-hardy annuals

Antirrhinum majus (snapdragon)

Cosmos bipinnatus (cosmos)

Didiscus coerulea 'Blue Lace' (blue laceflower)

Moluccella laevis (bells of Ireland)

Nicotiana alata 'Grandiflora' (tobacco plant)

Nicotiana sylvestris (tobacco plant)

Tropaeolum majus (nasturtium), e.g. 'Black Velvet'

Zinnia (zinnia)

Perennials

Agastache 'Blue Fortune' (Mexican giant hyssop)

Alcalthaea x *suffrutescens* 'Parkallee'
   (hollyhock/marshmallow cross)

Anemone japonica (Japanese anemone)

Aster x *frikartii* (Michaelmas daisy), e.g. 'Mönch'

Chrysanthemum (chrysanthemum), e.g. 'Allouise'

Cynara cardunculus (cardoon)

Dahlia (dahlia)

Delphinium (delphinium)

Dianthus (carnation)

Eupatorium (Joe Pye weed)

Foeniculum vulgare (fennel)

Gaura lindheimeri (gaura)

Hylotelephium spectabile (ice plant/sedum)

Knautia arvensis (field scabious)

Penstemon (beard tongue), e.g. 'Raven'

Persicaria bistorta (bistort), e.g. 'Superba'

Salvia (salvia), e.g. 'Amistad'

Salvia patens (gentian sage)

Salvia uliginosa (bog sage)

Thalictrum rochebruneanum (meadow rue)

Verbena bonariensis (Argentinian vervain)

Shrubs

Hydrangea arborescens 'Annabelle' (sevenbark)

Hydrangea macrophylla (mophead hydrangea)

Hydrangea paniculata (paniculate hydrangea)

Rosa (rose) – for flowers and hips

Climbers

Clematis tangutica (clematis), e.g. 'Bill Mackenzie'

Hedera helix (ivy)

Parthenocissus quinquefolia (Virginia creeper)

Rosa (rose)

At Henrietta's Cornish garden, Bokelly, the billowing border stays fresh in early autumn with bright-green euphorbia (*Euphorbia wallichii*). We also pick delicate spires of Culver's root (*Veronicastrum virginicum* 'Fascination'), meadow rue (*Thalictrum rochebruneanum*), phlox (*Phlox paniculata* 'Franz Schubert') and small magenta Carthusian pinks (*Dianthus carthusianorum*).

Opposite Dahlia 'Thomas Edison' grows in zinc pots on this London roof terrace, showing that you can gather cut flowers even from a small space. On the table is a vase of cosmos 'Dazzler': these last well in water and continue to flower if deadheaded in the vase.

Previous page, left Dahlias 'David Howard', 'Karma Choc' and 'Jowey Linda' in a silver sugar bowl.
Previous page, right We hated this red and yellow dahlia when it flowered and swore we had never ordered it, but florists loved it: more Van Gogh sunflower than dahlia.
Pages 144–145 Dahlias, from left to right in the vase: 'Labyrinth', 'Otto's Thrill', 'Edge of Joy', 'Wizard of Oz', 'Jowey Linda' and 'Santa Claus'.

Following page, left Dahlias 'Thomas Edison', 'Elma E' and 'Jowey Linda' in the hall, ready to be loaded into a van to head off to florists.
Following page, right Dahlias 'Thomas Edison' and 'Elma E' in the library with the teacup.
Pages 152–153 Market finds and a wall of random flower paintings by our children in the flower room.
Pages 154–155 Deep-red heads of sedum (*Hylotelephium spectabile*) and mophead hydrangeas (*Hydrangea macrophylla*) sit snuggly among lime-green hydrangea 'Annabelle' and wild, starry white asters. This aster has always been in the gardens at Wardington – it runs rampant and is good for cutting in the autumn.

Top left   Argentinian vervain (*Verbena bonariensis*) and hydrangea 'Annabelle' frame the steps on the bottom lawn.

Top right   Velvety snapdragons (*Antirrhinum majus*) last well in a vase.

Above left   Abyssinian gladiolus (*Gladiolus murielae*) exudes a heavenly scent.

Above right   Soft, creamy ice-cream ruffles of *Alcalthaea* x *suffrutescens* 'Parkallee' bring height to our borders and arrangements in autumn.

Top left Tiny cyclamens in a tiny cup. Autumn-flowering *Cyclamen hederifolium* likes to hide in the shade of the garden.

Top right A vase of dahlias (left) – 'Thomas Edison', 'Labyrinth' and 'Otto's Thrill' – takes afternoon tea with another vase of 'Café au Lait', 'Otto's Thrill' and 'Elma E', composing themselves before heading to a glamorous party in London.

Above left Dahlia 'Santa Claus' with morning tea in the garden.

Above right *Hydrangea paniculata* 'Kyushu' is full of movement, both in the garden and in a vase.

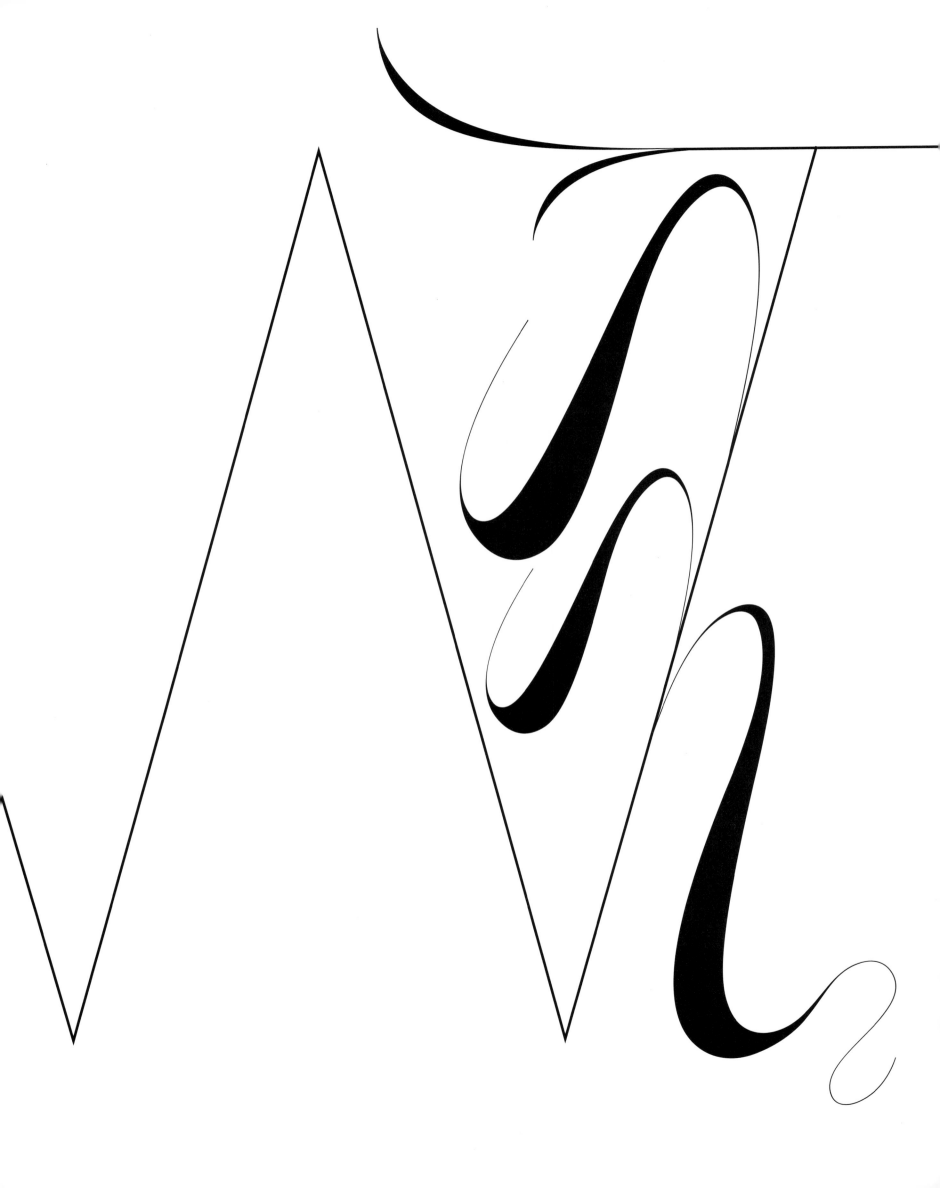

Winter

Don't think the garden loses its ecstasy in winter. It's quiet, but the roots are down there riotous.

Rumi

To do

WINTER

Under cover

Start to sow hardy annuals, e.g. sweet peas and Iceland poppies, in late winter.
Take root cuttings from perennials.
Continue planting paperwhites in pots, or among pebbles in shallow water, for a succession of flowers throughout winter.
Pot up snowdrops and winter aconites and bring them inside.
Pot up Christmas roses (*Helleborus niger*) and bring inside.
Bring rhododendron 'Fragrantissimum' inside in late winter.
Order seeds, as well as autumn- and winter-flowering bulbs, for the garden.

In the garden

Plant snowdrops 'in the green' (i.e. in growth) in late winter.
Cut back leaves of hellebores to show flowers.
Cut down perennial borders later in winter; lift and divide summer-flowering perennials.
Plant peonies and bare-root roses; prune roses and mulch with compost in late winter.
Cover rhubarb with terracotta forcing pots.
Prune hydrangeas (*Hydrangea arborescens* cultivars such as 'Annabelle' and paniculate varieties) in late winter.
Plant bare-root trees and shrubs; take hardwood cuttings from shrubs.
Try to grit the crowns of the delphiniums before stopping work for the holidays.

We pot up old willow pattern tureens with white hyacinths in winter.

To gather

Bulbs and corms

Bulbs for outside

Crocus (crocus), e.g. *Crocus tommassinianus* (early crocus)

Cyclamen coum (sowbread)

Eranthis hyemalis (winter aconite)

Galanthus (snowdrop), e.g. 'Sam Arnott'

Iris reticulata (early bulbous iris)

Narcissus (daffodil), e.g. 'Tête-à-Tête'

Bulbs for forcing inside

Crocus vernus (spring crocus), e.g. 'Jeanne d'Arc'

Hyacinthus orientalis (hyacinth), e.g. 'White Pearl'

Narcissus papyraceus (paperwhite), e.g. 'Bridal Crown' or 'Ziva'

Bulbs for potting up and bringing in from the garden

Eranthis hyemalis (winter aconite)

Galanthus (snowdrop)

Other plants for pots inside

Helleborus niger (Christmas rose)

Rhododendron 'Fragrantissimum' (rhododendron)

Perennials

Chrysanthemum (chrysanthemum), e.g. 'Denise Oatridge'

Helleborus argutifolius (Corsican hellebore)

Helleborus x *hybridus* (hybrid Lenten rose)

Helleborus niger (Christmas rose)

Rheum x *hybridum* (rhubarb) – forced

Climbers

Clematis vitalba (old man's beard)

Foliage

Bergenia (elephant's ear)

Camellia (camellia)

Crataegus (hawthorn) – for foliage and hips

Ilex aquifolium (holly)

Magnolia grandiflora (evergreen magnolia/bull bay)

Prunus laurocerasus (laurel)

Rosmarinus officinalis (rosemary)

Shrubs and trees

Camellia (camellia)

Chaenomeles (Japanese quince)

Daphne (daphne)

Hydrangea (hydrangea) – for seed heads

Ilex verticillata (winterberry)

Lonicera fragrantissima (winter-flowering honeysuckle)

Prunus x *subhirtella* (winter-flowering cherry)

Sarcococca confusa (sweet box)

Viburnum x *bodnantense* 'Dawn' (viburnum)

Henrietta's great-grandfather, Percy Dibley, started his plant nursery in West Sussex in the 1930s. His passion: chrysanthemums, rows and rows of prize-winning blooms. We are now taking up the mantle, experimenting with growing different varieties.
Opposite Pale-pink chrysanthemum 'Allouise' and viburnum (*Viburnum bodnantense* 'Dawn').

Previous page We are grateful to hellebores, which flower at a time when there is little in the garden. The hybrid Lenten rose (*Helleborus* x *hybridus*) can be tricky, but we find it lasts longer if picked when it is going to seed in late spring and its stems are seared in boiling water.
Pages 166–167 Tiny, bashful snowdrops (*Galanthus nivalis*) appear just as we are tiring of long, grey winter days.
Pages 164–165 The nun's bathing pool lies quietly in winter.

We pick blooms from the glorious, glossy, evergreen camellia 'Black Lace' in winter.

Opposite It is in winter that we are particularly thankful for the glossy leaves of the evergreen magnolia (*Magnolia grandiflora*), though it flowers sparingly in summer, and for the bright-green bracts of euphorbia (*Euphorbia characias* subsp. *wulfenii*).

Previous page, left Scented *Daphne odora* is lovely for a posy beside the bath or bed in winter.
Previous page, right Bright-yellow winter aconites (*Eranthis hyemalis*) are plucked from the cold woodland floor and brought into the flower room, ready to be potted up.

Following page Camellia 'Debbie' in a Wedgwood vase in the library. Camellias last a long time inside, and unopened buds will open in the warmth.

iving in Ireland

TASCHEN

E ENGLISH GARDEN

THAMES AND HUDSON

EONARDO DA V

Top left   The bold red berries of winterberry (*Ilex verticillata*) are striking and full of Christmas cheer.

Top right   When all is grey in the garden, the delicious fragrance of daphne (*Daphne odora*) will surprise and uplift you.

Above left   Dried heads of hydrangea 'Annabelle' last throughout the winter.

Above right   We force rhubarb by covering it with terracotta forcing pots. Here we sent bowls of it, along with bowls of mint grown in the glasshouse, to Soane Britain for the launch of their fabric 'Botanic Garden' – the colourways of which were rhubarb and mint.

Top left A small dried branch of the strawberry tree (*Arbutus unedo*) sits on a mantelpiece.
Top right In the winter we pot up snowdrops (*Galanthus nivalis*) and winter aconites (*Eranthis hyemalis*) from the garden to bring into the house.
Above left Throughout autumn and early winter we pot up bulbs of crocus 'Jeanne d'Arc', which appear like white candles out of the dark soil.
Above right Rhododendron 'Fragrantissimum' floods the hall with its heady scent in late winter.

Your Cut Flower Garden

Making Flower Beds

If you are creating your beds from an existing area of lawn or grass, we recommend taking off the top 2 centimetres (1 inch) of soil with a turf cutter to remove the turf and existing seed bed. You can then plant in rows 60–120 centimetres (2–3 feet) wide, i.e. once or twice the width of a broadfork, with narrow walking paths of 25–60 centimetres (1–2 feet) depending on the spread of the plants. It is important to have access for picking the flowers, so you won't need to walk on the growing beds, as this compacts the soil. We also like to cover any bare soil between plants with green manures (see page 188) or mulch, to protect the light- and heat-sensitive microorganisms in the soil. Weed-control matting can work brilliantly for well-organised growers, but we prefer having the flexibility to add more compost and/or plant green manures to feed the soil life throughout the growing season.

Protecting the Beds

It makes life much easier if you can find or create a space for your flower beds that is protected from the wind and roaming wildlife. Walled gardens are perfect for this, as their stone and brick walls harness the heat and keep predators at bay. Hedging on its own, or ideally with a netting fence hidden inside it, can also work well, since you can play with the height and shape to obtain the effect you want. You just have to be careful that the hedge's roots are kept in check, so as not to rob the beds of moisture and nutrients. Woven willow or hazel fences make a lovely natural alternative, but will need replacing after several years.

Edging the Beds

It is important to consider how to protect the edges of the beds, particularly from encroaching lawn. Timber has to be untreated if it surrounds anything edible, and you need to keep in mind that it will rot over time. If metal is your choice, it needs to be of good quality and flush with the lawn for ease of mowing. Mild steel is a good choice (approximately 6–10 millimetres thick by 100 millimetres deep); we like the way it rusts and bends to create fluid curves. Edging flower beds with flagstones also makes cutting lawns easier – as often the foliage invades the grass, and it is tricky to mow when clouds of catmint are languishing on the lawn. Using plants like box (*Buxus sempervirens*), euphorbia (*Euphorbia oblongata*), parsley (*Petroselinum*), myrtle (*Myrtus communis* subsp. *tarentina*), lavender (*Lavandula angustifolia*), hedge germander (*Teucrium* x *lucidrys*) and common lady's mantle (*Alchemilla vulgaris*) to edge your beds allows you to pick many of them to use as cut flowers or herbs.

Paths

We are lucky to have many old stone paths at Wardington – we let seeds run rampant between the cracks and just strim the plants when they get out of control. Gravel and hoggin (a compacted mix of clay, sand, gravel and granite dust) paths reflect the light on grey days, but they are also effectively a seed bed and unless you want to spray them – which we don't – can be time-consuming to weed. We try to hoe any gravel paths regularly. Occasionally, we take out the butane torch, which is on wheels, and burn the weeds off the paths – but this rather ferocious beast often stretches its hot tongue around some of the plants inside the beds! Over time, we have let many of the paths revert to grass as it is the easiest to maintain when grown on a well-drained base, although less good when it rains. Brick paths are also pretty, but can be slippery in wet weather.

Compost

For your flowering plants to thrive, you need healthy soil, and the way to achieve this is to feed and nurture the microorganisms in the soil by adding compost. We have started a new system of creating compost windrows to make high-quality microbially active compost. It is sometimes tricky to find a spot that is just right for compost. It needs to be close enough for easy access, but tucked away out of sight. Try to find an area that is sheltered and with room for a few bays, or piles of material waiting to be made into compost, and enough space for two or three windrows – the minimum size for a windrow is 1 metre (about 3 feet) long by 1 metre wide and 1 metre high.

We use three bays to separate the various ingredients for our compost: one bay has farmyard manure and bedding from the stables (mixed nitrogen and carbon), the next is full of green garden waste and lawn clippings (high in nitrogen) and another is full of old leaves and dead woody waste (high in carbon). We then create windrows about 3 metres (10 feet) long, 2 metres (6 feet) wide at the base and 1.2 metres (4 feet) high. These Toblerone-shaped piles are formed from alternating layers of nitrogen-rich material (clippings from the garden, weeds and manure) and carbon-rich materials (straw, leaves and young woody stems) with water added to each layer to make sure the compost is about 55–60 per cent moisture (above left). To finish we add 10 per cent clay, plus a microbial inoculant (a mix of eighty-four different microbes) or biodynamic preparations or 10 per cent of some existing compost to serve as an activator, then we turn the lot with forks to aerate and mix everything together (above right). This cocktail of ingredients triggers the process of decomposition. The windrows are then covered in a breathable membrane such as Toptex that keeps out rain and sunlight but allows the microbes to breathe.

The same process works on a smaller scale and without any manure: household kitchen waste is a good source of nitrogen, and cardboard provides carbon as it breaks down. People often ask if plants like dock, bindweed and ground elder can go into compost. We do include these as the high temperatures generated in the windrows kills them, but if in doubt keep them out. Remember that the more diversity there is in the compost, the happier the microbes are – much like our own gut flora.

We want the right levels of oxygen, water and food, and the optimum temperature, for our teams of microorganisms to break down the organic matter and form a high-quality humus brimming with life. As soon as the temperature reaches 59°C (138°F), we turn the compost to ensure that any weed seeds and harmful bacteria are killed. Over the next five to ten days, we turn the compost between three and five times and keep checking the temperature – if the temperature exceeds 65°C (149°F), the beneficial microbes start to die. During this time we also monitor levels of carbon dioxide with a meter to ensure there is enough oxygen in the windrow – this is not essential, but we find it helps to keep the compost in optimum condition. Each time we turn the windrow, we add water if it is dry (ideally rain or chemical-free water). Turning a windrow is much easier than turning a large pile of compost, but if you do decide to stick with static piles, make sure they are layered with carbon- and nitrogen-rich materials, and keep them moist and aerated by turning as regularly as you can.

When the compost starts to cool (usually after a week to ten days), we leave it until it is at ambient temperature and fully broken down. In this way we can make high-quality, fully digested, microbially rich compost in six to eight weeks. This may seem like a lot of work – but the reward is worth it: well-balanced compost that is free of weed seeds saves you time in the garden, as your plants will be healthy and resilient.

Liquid Feeds

We use liquid feeds and compost teas throughout the growing season as they contain many important plant nutrients beneficial to both plants and soil health. To make our own liquid feeds or teas, we put a variety of greens – such as comfrey, nettles and weeds – in bags made from fine-mesh mutton cloth (also called stockinette), then leave them to soak in buckets or large barrels of rainwater (to avoid the chlorine that's generally added to the mains water supply), ideally with taps at the bottom. We also steep them directly in water (above right) – but crucially, before doing this, we make sure the plants are not seeding. We work on the basis of two watering cans of rainwater to a bucket of greens, covering them to contain the smell (caused by the activity of anaerobic bacteria) and stirring occasionally. After four weeks, we strain off the nutrient-rich liquid, diluting it to a ratio of roughly 1:10 with rainwater. We then fill a watering or backpack sprayer and spray the soil when we plant seedlings, and also spray the leaves of growing plants.

Nettles are packed with nutrients and particularly high in nitrogen, so we often use nettle tea on our dahlias during the growing season. Borage, too, makes a nitrogen-rich tea. Comfrey is a good source of trace elements, including nitrogen, phosphorus and particularly potassium, the latter being good for flowers, seed and fruit. We grow 'Bocking 14' comfrey (*Symphytum* x *uplandicum* 'Bocking 14') for making liquid feeds, as it is higher in nutrients than common comfrey and does not seed around the garden – just be careful to wear gloves when picking it, as its bristly leaves can irritate the skin. We have also tried simply packing comfrey leaves into a bucket without any water and collecting the run-off, which should be diluted with rainwater before use to a ratio of 1:20. In summer, we like to add a handful of magnesium-rich Epsom salts to bathwater, pouring it out of the window onto the climbing plants below afterwards.

Magnesium is vital for making chlorophyll, which plants need for photosynthesis, and so this is particularly good for turning yellowing plants green (above left). We also make biodynamic preparations for the garden, including 507 Valerian Preparation, which we spray on our compost windrows (above middle) – it is supposed to stimulate microorganisms and make phosphorus more available to plants.

If you are unlucky enough to have the invasive common horsetail (*Equisetum arvense*) growing in your garden, console yourself by using it as a tea. Boil its stems in water for twenty minutes, then leave the infusion to cool before using it diluted at a ratio of 1:10 as an anti-fungal foliar feed, particularly on young seedlings to prevent them damping off. Chamomile tea has a similar effect. After a day's weeding, we often use a mix of weeds to make liquid feeds, particularly those weeds with long tap roots like borage, dock, plantain, yarrow and burdock, as their leaves are rich in a wide variety of plant nutrients. Dandelion is high in iron, and even the dreaded couch grass is rich in potassium and silica. We also use seaweed tea for its high nutrient value.

Finally, we scale up our compost by making compost tea. We put a handful of microbially rich compost into our compost-tea maker with a compost-tea activator and let it brew for twenty-four hours, during which time the mix is gently aerated, keeping the microbes alive and helping them to proliferate. We use the resulting compost tea on the soil when planting seedlings and every couple of weeks as a foliar spray while the plants are growing.

Green Manures

These quick-growing plants improve soil fertility and structure, suppress weeds and often attract beneficial insects. We plant a variety of green manures for different purposes in our cut-flower and vegetable beds.

Sometimes we dig the mature plants directly into the soil, approximately 15 centimetres (6 inches) deep, as long as they are not too leggy to decompose quickly, then we allow four weeks before we plant again. At other times, in order to avoid disturbing the soil, and where time is of the essence, we cut the plants down to use in our compost and simply plant new seedlings directly among the leftover stubble.

To prevent weed growth and keep soil microorganisms alive and well-fed, we are always keen to avoid bare earth, so throughout the year we keep a supply of green manure seeds ready to sow as and when an area is to be left fallow. In spring we like to plant fast-growing green manures like mustard (*Sinapis alba*); fiddleneck (*Phacelia tanacetifolia*), above far left; and buckwheat (*Fagopyrum esculentum*), above middle left, where we will later grow half-hardy annuals such as cosmos after the first frosts are over. We take care not to let the mustard go to seed, digging it in as soon as the first flowers show. However, we are always reluctant to cut down the beautiful white flowers of buckwheat and the lilac-blue phacelia/fiddleneck once they are alive with bees, often leaving them to attract pollinators to the garden.

Throughout summer we are quick to fill in areas left by harvested rows of vegetables or flowers with 'catch crops' of green manures until we plant again. And as winter approaches we sow grazing rye (*Secale cereale*), winter vetch (*Vicia sativa*) or field beans (*Vicia faba*) to keep the soil covered, digging them into the soil in spring. Allow a month between digging in grazing rye and replanting the bed, as the decomposing rye releases a substance that can inhibit the germination of some seeds. Last year we sowed field beans over some of our rows of tulips (above middle) – not only did this suppress the germination of spring weeds, it also gave a lush green backdrop to the tulips as they grew. Once the tulips had flowered, we scythed down the field beans and planted cosmos among their roots.

The advantage of green manures from the legume (pea and bean) family, such as clover, field beans and vetch, is that they absorb nitrogen from the air and fix it in nodules on their roots, making it available to the soil as they die back. To improve the soil and keep weeds at bay, we often underplant our rows of sweet peas with crimson clover (*Trifolium incarnatum*), which provides a frothing red skirt to their teepee of bamboo stakes (above far right). And in areas where we are keen to make a longer-term investment to improve soil quality, we plant red clover (*Trifolium pratense*), which will grow for up to two years, smothering weeds and fixing nitrogen in the soil. We also often turn to lupins, with their deep tap roots, to help fix nitrogen and open up the structure of sandy soils.

Green Manures

	SOW	SOIL	GROW
Vetch (tare) *Vicia villosa* – winter vetch *Vicia sativa* – summer vetch Hardy annual	July–September, March–May Winter 2.5g per m² Summer 16g per m²	Avoid acid and dry soils; likes heavier soils	2–3 months
Crimson clover *Trifolium incarnatum* Hardy annual	March–August Broadcast (3g per m²) and sow at a shallow depth	Prefers sandy soil or good loam	2–3 months, may over-winter
Fenugreek *Trigonella foenum-graecum* Half-hardy annual	March–August Broadcast (5g per m²) or sow in 15cm rows	Well-drained but moist soil	2–3 months
Yellow trefoil (black medick) *Medicago lupulina* Hardy biennial	March–August Broadcast lightly (1g per m²)	Will stand dry light soil, but not acid	3 months plus
Mustard *Sinapis alba* Half-hardy annual	March–September Broadcast (5g per m²) or sow in 15cm rows	Prefers fertile soil	1–2 months
Fiddleneck/Phacelia *Phacelia tanacetifolia* Hardy annual	March–September Broadcast (2g per m²) or sow in 20cm rows	Most soils, especially dry ones	1–3 months
Alfalfa (lucerne) *Medicago sativa* Hardy perennial	April–July Broadcast (2g per m²)	Avoid acid, wet soils; prefers dry soils	1 year plus
Buckwheat *Fagopyrum esculentum* Hardy annual	April–August Best sown in rows 20cm apart (6g per m²)	Tolerates poor soil; not good on heavy soil	1–3 months
Red clover *Trifolium pratense* Hardy perennial	April–August Broadcast (3g per m²) and sow at a shallow depth; too deep will reduce germination	All soils	3–18 months
Rye, Hungarian grazing *Secale cereale* Hardy annual	August–November Broadcast (16g per m²) or sow in 20cm rows	Most soils; copes well with clay	Over winter
Beans, field or broad *Vicia faba* Hardy annual	September–November Allow 10cm between beans, in rows 15–20cm apart	Likes heavy soil; tolerates lighter soil if moist	Over winter

NOTES

Winter hairy vetch is frost-tolerant so provides good winter cover. Summer vetch has heavy foliage to suppress weeds. Both are good nitrogen fixers as members of the legume family. Root system is shallow but can reach 2 metres (6 feet) in length. Winter vetch is good for preventing nitrogen leaching in winter. Do not plant with peonies as can carry botrytis. Dig in before flowering and allow one month before sowing other seeds (as it releases a substance that inhibits growth of small seeds).

Vigorous and brilliant for smothering weeds and fixing nitrogen. Wonderful crimson flowers which are loved by bees. It has deep roots. May over-winter in milder areas, but if not it can be dug in the following spring.

Provides a quick boost to soil fertility in just a few months. Rapidly provides a lot of foliage, very good at suppressing weeds.

A low-growing green manure which is useful for under-sowing taller crops such as climbing beans – once beans are approximately 15cm high. A legume, so good for fixing nitrogen. Yellow flowers attract bees and beneficial insects, but sets seed rapidly, so dig in promptly.

A fast-growing green manure which can reach 60–90cm in four to eight weeks, when it should be chopped down and incorporated into the soil. A vigorous weed suppressant. A brassica, so should not be sown where club root is suspected. May need water to help it establish.

A fast grower and good weed suppressant. Needs dark to germinate. Pretty lavender-blue flowers are very attractive to bees and beneficial insects. Breaks down quickly when dug in due to fine leaf structure. Good to combine with buckwheat, annual clovers and mustard.

The cut foliage acts as a mulch, and the deep tap root helps sort out compacted soil. Needs a bacteria – rhizobium – present in soil to nodulate then fix nitrogen – purchase this to add at time of sowing.

Grows fast. Takes up phosphate and then disperses it in the soil after digging in. Large leaves suppress weeds, and white flowers attract beneficial insects. Thought to produce toxic substances that inhibit the growth of other seeds, so leave a month before planting seeds after digging in – seedlings are not affected by it.

Lasts for two years or more. Should be cut regularly, whenever it reaches a height of 30cm, and used as a mulch. Its deep roots are good for improving soil structure and binding together light soils, helping to prevent nitrogen leaching in winter.

One of the best green manures for over-wintering. Excellent soil improver, particularly for clay soils. Grows throughout winter and is frost-tolerant. Can be difficult to dig in in the spring. Releases substances that inhibit seed germination, so allow four weeks before sowing seeds – seedlings are not affected.

Easily grown bean. Best sown in alternate rows with grazing rye to improve weed control. The root nodules fix nitrogen, but to capture it, be sure to dig in before seeds (i.e. beans) form.

The Potting Shed

There is nothing quite like the feeling of walking into a potting shed: the smell of damp earth, the coolness of the air, and rows of pots waiting to be filled with seeds and cuttings. Our potting shed at Wardington has the added benefit of a roaring fire – so cheerful in the winter months when we are making wreaths and dividing dahlias. It is great to have a waist-high bench for potting up seeds, or potting on seedlings and perennials that have been lifted and divided from the borders. Dividing perennials and taking hard and soft wood cuttings and root cuttings is an inexpensive way to increase your plants each year.

We like to have a good mix of small and medium-sized pots on hand, as well as some large pots for perennials that have been divided and need to be moved to the nursery. We would love to use only old terracotta pots, but in reality we use lots of plastic pots that our plants have been delivered in over the years.

The ideal composition of the potting mix depends on what you are sowing or growing. We usually make our own mix from compost, sand and molehills (gathered over winter), using more sand in seed trays and more compost when potting on into larger pots to supply the extra nutrients plants need to grow and develop.

As a general rule you should plant a seed at a depth three times its size. Make sure you follow the instructions on the seed package; some seeds need light to germinate, as this helps to break their dormancy, and some like it dark. For seeds that need light to germinate (such as poppies, snapdragons and geraniums), we sprinkle a light dusting of vermiculite over the seeds or just press them lightly onto the surface of the soil and keep them moist. For those that like to be tucked up in the dark, we sieve potting mix over the top and then cover them to block the light, checking regularly for germination and removing the cover when we see the first shoots. When the seedlings have developed their first two to five leaves or when they are big enough to handle, we prick them out into small pots to grow on, ready to be planted out in the garden.

Always water everything in well, using a watering can with a fine rose for seeds and delicate seedlings. We have a couple of water butts to collect the rainwater that runs off the glasshouse roof – this is brilliant for watering seedlings as it is free from chlorine.

Under Cover

Although having somewhere to grow plants under cover is not strictly necessary, it really helps to extend the season in cooler climates. We have a rather tired old glasshouse that is constantly losing panes of glass, some cold frames, and a long polytunnel, where we have had success with tulips, Iceland poppies, ranunculus, sweet peas, delphiniums, dahlias and zinnias. We have also grown some cosmos – which grows tall and leggy but is great for large arrangements for events. (In hindsight, it would have been better to have a Spanish polytunnel where you can roll up the sides on hot summer days, to allow more air to circulate.)

The glasshouse oscillates between faithful friend and health hazard. No one is allowed in there when the winds get up. One end is lined with bubble wrap for extra insulation, and we heat it during frosts – this is where we protect tender perennials (such as pelargoniums, salvia 'Amistad' and rhododendron 'Fragrantissimum') over the winter, and is also

where we keep the propagator we use to root cuttings and germinate seeds. The other half of the glasshouse accommodates an old grapevine and is where we grow tomatoes in summer and semi-hardy plants waiting to be planted out in spring.

We have also made some cold frames out of timber, with lids of clear plastic sheeting. These are brilliant for hardening off seedlings – preparing them for life outside after their warm, controlled life under glass. They spend up to a week adjusting before being planted out. If you don't have a glasshouse, cold frames give tender plants some protection.

Staking and Supports

Part of growing flowers is knowing when and how to stake the more willowy of our friends. We generally find that if we plant the flowers slightly closer than their maximum spread, they will hold each other up – but every plant is different, and there are many ways to keep them upright and happy.

Mostly, we use bamboo canes or hazel stakes threaded with twine alongside each row, and occasionally we run a length of twine across the row to hold individual plants upright (above left). We avoid using plastic mesh because it always seems to become tied up with the plants and difficult to remove at the end of the season.

For sweet peas, we use teepees made from bamboo canes (above right), and for some of the very lax or large roses, metal supports work well. Our dahlias are individually staked with three bamboo stakes encircled in twine, as are the tall delphiniums.

We do not stake peonies when they are planted in rows, as they tend to support each other, but in the borders we give them a helping hand with metal hoops.

Collecting Seed

Once you can feel the summer cooling, husks start forming on the plants – the buzz and hum of languid days is replaced by a gentle rustling sound, as the seeds swell and their casings dry out. It never fails to amaze us that flowers which have already given us such joy all summer are still willing to give up their seed so that the whole wonderful display can continue again next year. We collect our own seed each year or, for plants we haven't grown before, we look for suppliers of organic or heirloom seeds. We try to avoid buying F1 hybrid seeds – created in a controlled environment, these are designed to be sterile, so you cannot collect seed from them for the next growing season.

Filling envelopes and little brown paper bags with seeds is so rewarding, labelling them with pencil in the top right-hand corner and then storing them in lidded metal boxes to save them from being eaten by hungry mice in winter. Placing these in our cool, dark seed room with its slate benches and tiled walls feels deeply satisfying: all that beauty

and knowledge is stored in an assortment of shapes and sizes, from minute poppy seeds to the bullet-shaped seeds of sweet peas, from the feathered seeds of black salsify to the pinched seedcases of buckwheat and bells of Ireland. This year we collected dahlia seed for the first time. The intense coral-pink petals dried like shards of silk (above).

This whole topic is worthy of another book, one we might just write one day. Nature has a unique and multifaceted way of reproducing itself, and intrinsic to a plant's biological makeup is the wisdom of how to grow – some of which we understand after centuries of botanical study, but much of which is still a mystery. The plant and animal kingdoms are so interconnected that the more seeds are manipulated or modified, the less information they have to communicate with the rest of the natural world.

Our Favourite Tools

Having the right tools makes all the difference, and well-designed tools are a real pleasure to use.

WOLF-Garten hoe
This meaty hoe is the one we use to tackle tough weeds.

Copper hoe
A light and nimble hoe that's great for maintaining beds – we hoe every two weeks even before we see a slight flush of green, to prevent weeds taking hold. The copper is said to deter slugs.

Copper spade
Light and sharp, this spade glides into the soil.

Pitchfork
A pitchfork is brilliant for turning compost.

Great Dixter border fork
A small, dynamic and precise fork for any tricky areas.

Nunki weeder
A hand-held, agile copper tool for weeding intricate areas.

Copper trowel
A sharp, precise trowel with just the right angle and weight in the hand is invaluable in the potting shed and the garden.

Niwaki hori hori
We use this brilliant Japanese tool for everything from digging out tough weeds and removing ivy off walls to making holes for planting seedlings.

Bulb planter
An invaluable tool for the speedy planting of bulbs.

Niwaki topiary shears
These are wonderful for shaping topiary and for chopping up stems for compost.

Felco secateurs
It is essential to have clean secateurs that can be easily resharpened.

Broadfork
This is amazing for aerating the soil without disturbing it too much: use your body weight to make light work of heavy soils.

Garden sieves
We use these for grading compost and preparing seed trays.

Tamper
A small piece of flat wooden board with a handle on top for gently tamping down the soil before sowing.

Growing Cut Flowers

We leave pink peony poppies (*Papaver somniferum* var. *paeoniflorum*) to self-seed around the walled garden in high summer. The yellow flowers of black salsify (*Scorzonera hispanica*) add an unusual flash of vibrancy to an arrangement.

ach year at The Land Gardeners we trial new varieties of plants. Here we show you our favourite cut flowers which have performed well over time in these trials and which we have grown to love. They will all grow well in temperate climates. Those that will be most suitable for a hot climate are as follows: Roses (all), dahlias (all), bulbs and corms (*Allium* 'Purple Sensation', *Lilium regale*, *Ranunculus*), annuals (*Alcalthaea* x *suffrutescens* 'Parkallee', *Antirrhinum*, *Cosmos*, *Echium vulgare*, *Scabiosa caucasica*, *Papaver nudicaule* 'Champagne bubbles', *Nigella*, *Zinnia*), perennials (*Linaria purpurea* 'Canon Went', *Cephalaria gigantea*, *Centranthus lecoqii*, *Iris*, *Nepeta*, *Verbena bonariensis*), foliage (*Cynara cardunculus*, *Euphorbia characias* subsp. *wulfenii*, *Rosmarinus officinalis*) and trees and shrubs (*Magnolia grandiflora*).

Roses

Roses are not the longest-lasting cut flowers, but we have fallen under the spell of their beguiling fragrance, their soft, plump petals that float down to the floor. We grow many roses for the sheer romance of them. Most are English shrub roses, but we are now coming round to the charms of hybrid tea roses, the flowers of our grandmothers – starting out all crisp and perfect on their uptight bushes and ending up full, languid and blowsy, their petals crinkling like tissue, their colour more intense. They add energy and intensity to a bunch of English shrub roses.

Roses are amazing for events or for filling the house, instantly giving a home the feeling of being loved and lived in. Timeless and evocative of long, warm summer days, they settle the soul. We even grow once-blooming old shrub roses for their scent, natural movement and romantic, otherworldly air. Long boughs of these are brilliant to decorate an arch in a church, to drape over a long staircase or to soften a large urn of flowers.

We also love our climbing roses and have covered these, along with our other favourite climbers, on page 244.

Planting, Pruning and Feeding

It is best to plant roses in winter, and it is most economical to choose bare-root plants (these are sold without any soil, which makes them lighter to transport). You can technically plant potted roses all year round, but we believe it causes less stress if they are planted while they are dormant in the winter.

In brief, soak the bare roots in water for a couple of hours before planting. Dig a hole big enough to hold the rose so that the base of its stem is 5 centimetres (2 inches) below the top of the hole. Take the rose out of the water and lightly trim its roots, then sprinkle the base and sides of the hole with mycorrhizal funghi – this aids the uptake of water and nutrients, and can also act as a buffer against certain pathogens that may have been left behind in the soil if it has previously been used to grow roses. Position the rose centrally in the hole and hold it in place while you fill the hole with soil and compost. Water it in well. Once planted, it is a good idea to prune the rose for shape and shorten each stem to an outward-facing bud.

We lightly prune our roses in late autumn to help prevent windrock during winter storms. Then we prune them properly in early spring, cutting back the stems by a third for repeat-flowering and once-blooming shrub roses, and two thirds for hybrid tea and floribunda roses. We cut out any diseased, damaged or dead stems, then choose the strongest shoots to form the main framework of the rose.

We mulch our roses in spring with compost, and then again after their first flowering. We have found that spraying them with liquid seaweed and compost tea in spring and summer is useful as a foliar feed, and appears to help with fungal black spot and aphids. Diluted washing-up liquid is also good for attacking aphids.

Picking

Try not to pick roses on a wet day, as rain damages their petals. In fact, some growers plant their roses under cover to keep the rain off. We don't, but then we have to accept that some years will not be as bountiful as others. A lot of the time, the stems are quite short, so we put roses in little silver jugs or small glass or clay bottles, to sit on tables among candlesticks and glasses, or to place beside the bed or a bath. They look especially lovely when mixed with peonies or Iceland poppies.

We pick *Rosa mundi* for its fleeting beauty. Although it is not long-lasting in the vase, we are seduced by its stripes and its romantic history as a twelfth-century rose named after Rosamund, mistress of Henry II.

Alexander

Lady of Megginch

Princess Alexandra
of Kent

Boscobel

Gertrude Jekyll

Blessings

Royal Jubilee

Ferdinand Pichard

Duchess of Cornwall

Claire Austin

The Shepherdess

Geoff Hamilton

Wedgwood

Jude The Obscure

Sally Holmes

x odorata
Mutabilis

Shairfa Asma

Aphrodite

Peonies

Glamorous, abundant peonies: all Hollywood charisma and alluring folds of silk. No other flower is as seductive. While tree peonies have an exotic elegance in the garden, it is the herbaceous peonies (both lactifloras and hybrids) that are the best for cut flowers – and, once established in your garden, they will live for years.

Peonies are often viewed as a fleeting pleasure, but we extend our season by planting several different varieties, allowing us to cut armfuls of blooms for a good six weeks from late spring to early summer. They are to the world of flowers what Christian Dior's 'New Look' was to fashion: a young, full-skirted silhouette of exuberance, bursting with energy and confidence. We grow the doubles for their profusion of silky petals, and singles for their delicate tissue-paper petals that glow with a youthful luminescence. They are both voluptuous and generous, many even turning heads with their delicious fragrance.

Planting

Peonies like sun and humus-rich, well-drained soil. They are easy to grow. Plant them in winter, digging a hole and adding compost. Cover the base of the buds ('eyes') with no more than 5 centimetres (2 inches) of soil, to allow the winter cold to stimulate their flower buds – plant too deep and your peony will not flower.

Planting distance depends on the ultimate size of the peony. In general, most herbaceous perennials can be planted 75 centimetres (30 inches) apart, although we would allow at least 100 centimetres (40 inches) between the larger varieties, such as 'Coral Charm' and 'Pink Hawaiian Coral'. If you are planting them in a herbaceous bed, do not let them be crowded out by neighbours.

It is essential that the leaves of peonies get as much sun as possible, as this is the key way the tuber gains its energy for next year's blooms, so it is important not to cut down the dying leaves until they are completely brown in late summer. One way to distract your eye from the dying foliage is to interplant them with airy, feathery-leaved plants like dill (*Anethum graveolens*), cosmos and Argentinian vervein (*Verbena bonariensis*).

Picking

Initially you need to be patient. In the first year, just pick off any flower buds, leaving as much foliage as possible to enable the plant to store energy for the following year. Keep the plants well-watered, and your patience will soon be rewarded: after three to five years, you'll be picking armfuls of extravagant blooms that can last up to fourteen days in water.

Pick peonies when the buds feel like marshmallows – soft and squidgy when squeezed – and they will open in the vase. Avoid picking stems any longer than the distance from your elbow to your fingertips, to ensure sufficient foliage is left on the plant. Do not pick peonies on a wet day.

A bowl of early-flowering peonies: 'Chippewa', 'Gladys McArthur' and 'Coral Charm'. It is a wonderful moment in late winter when the first pink buds of the early-flowering peonies peek through the brown soil, swelling with expectant growth and willing us to hold on through the grey days of winter with the promise that summer will return.

Following page Our favourite peonies, flowering in the early (left two columns), middle (middle two columns) and late (right two columns) parts of the season.

Bowl of Cream

Peach Mist

Festiva Maxima

Pink Hawaiian
Coral

Miss America

Gardenia

Paula Fay

Coral Charm

Kelway's Glorious

Monsieur Jules
Elie

Nick Shaylor

Mother's Choice

Vogue

Solange

Pillow Talk

Karl Rosenfield

Dr Alexander
Fleming

My Pal Rudy

Dahlias

Years ago we spotted dinner plate dahlias in a potager in the Pays de la Loire region of France, their magnificent heads of furling pink petals standing tall among the vegetables. We were captivated, and soon found ourselves digging out two new borders, each 50 metres (about 165 feet) long, to house our new collection: mainly dinner plates, a few pompoms and the odd collarette. Now rows of hot-coloured dahlias, including deep-pink 'Elma E', velvet-purple 'Thomas Edison' and fiery orange 'Eileen', stand next to the cool clotted creams of 'Café au Lait' and 'Peaches and Cream', and our favourite red-and-white striped bloom, 'Santa Claus'.

The Victorians loved these Mexican fireworks of the flower world, planting them en masse in bedding schemes. However, they fell out of favour – considered too crude and vulgar for the naturalistic herbaceous borders of the twentieth-century English country garden. A loyal band of growers still carried a torch for them, showing their increasingly bright and brash blooms at horticultural shows. But now they are back and have resumed their rightful place in our gardens. Flamboyant flowers held high above their leaves provide a thrilling energy and colour in late summer and into autumn that is unsurpassed by any other flower. As Gertrude Jekyll observed in 1899, 'The dahlia's first duty in life is to flaunt and to swagger and to carry gorgeous blooms well above its leaves and on no account to hang its head.'

Planting and Staking

To get a head start, we sprout some of our dahlias in pots in spring, keeping them well-watered in a frost-free glasshouse or polytunnel. The advantages of doing this are that the shoots are established before the slugs can find them, and we can take root cuttings from them to increase our stock. However, with the majority of our dahlias, we wait until the frosts are over and then plant them directly into the beds, which are well-drained – although they are thirsty, dahlias don't like to sit in water – and in full sun. We always tie a label to each tuber before we bury it beneath the soil, so we'll know what variety it is when we lift it at the end of the season. We dig a large hole, approximately 30 centimetres (12 inches) deep, add compost and tip in a bucketful of water to thoroughly wet the soil – this allows us to check that there is good drainage and also really helps to kick-start the dahlia's growth.

Check the spread of each dahlia to work out how far apart to plant them: we normally plant our large dinner plate dahlias 80 centimetres (about 30 inches) apart in rows, allowing approximately 1 metre (3 feet) between the rows to give us room for picking.

If you have a problem with slugs, treat your dahlia bed with nematodes six weeks before planting, at the time of planting, and again six weeks later. Alternatively, you can try circling the dahlias with coarse grit around the stems, using beer traps, and venturing into the garden at night with a torch to pick off the slugs by hand.

We put a 1.5-metre (5-foot) hazel or bamboo stake in the ground by each plant. If the soil is dry and the weather is warm, make sure you give the tubers a further water – and if you are in a drought-prone area, it is a good idea to make an indentation in the soil around the stems to create a shallow 'bowl' that will collect water when it rains. Keep an eye on the weather too: it's vital to water your dahlias regularly for the first three weeks if there isn't a lot of rain.

When our dinner plate dahlias reach knee height, we push in two additional 1.5-metre (5-foot) stakes around the plant and wrap twine around all three stakes. As the plants grow taller, we add further lengths of twine at 45-centimetre (1-foot) intervals – we normally end up with about three lots of twine – enough to hold up the plant if it's windy and the flowers are particularly heavy. We follow the same principle with smaller dahlias, though the plants won't grow as high. Once they are up and growing, keep dahlias well-watered and spray with liquid seaweed or another foliar feed regularly. Dahlias are heavy feeders, requiring a steady supply of water and food to support their extraordinary growth.

If you find you have a problem with earwigs, put a small terracotta pot upside down on a bamboo or hazel stake and tuck some straw into it: the earwigs crawl inside to nest, so make sure you check the pot and clear them out regularly. Thrips, tiny winged insects that damage leaves by sucking out the juices, can also be troublesome. The best way to deal with these is to spray them with diluted washing-up liquid.

Picking, Lifting and Dividing

When picking dahlias, we try to cut back to either a bud or the main stem, to allow further buds to continue growing. Remember that dahlia buds will not open once picked, so you need to pick them when the flowers are opening.

After the first frost, when the dahlia leaves have turned black, cut them right down to 10 centimetres (4 inches) off the ground. Interestingly, the cold prompts the dahlias to produce 'eyes' (growth buds) at the base of the stem, which will form the impetus for the following year's growth.

If you live in a climate where the temperature rarely falls below 5°C (41°F), you can just leave the tubers in the ground and mulch them with well-rotted compost and straw. If your soil is heavy and prone to waterlogging, or you live in a cold climate, then you should lift your dahlia tubers. We always try to lift them after a dry spell, so the tubers are cleaner and there is less disturbance to the soil.

Check that they are still labelled – otherwise it is very easy to confuse them – then wash them and store them upside down on their stalks to dry in a glasshouse or frost-free shed, ideally in a spot where they'll get some warmth from the sun. When they are dry, pack them into labelled crates full of straw to keep them in the dark and store in a cool, dry, frost-free potting shed or garage for the winter, checking that the mice do not nibble them.

We tend not to divide the tubers at this stage, as they often separate naturally over winter. We wait instead until the spring, when we divide them into smaller pieces, making sure each one has an eye (there will be more tubers than eyes), and discarding any damaged or broken tubers. If they are not already sprouting, we often place the tubers in a warm place for a few days to see which eyes are viable and begin to sprout.

Santa Claus

There are nine types of dahlias, all with varied characteristics: single, waterlily, collarette, anemone, pompom, ball, semi-cactus, cactus and decorative (plus a tenth miscellaneous type). We particularly love decorative or dinner plate dahlias, whose flamboyant, large blooms can reach up to 30 centimetres in diameter, e.g. 'Elma E', 'Otto's Thrill' and 'Café au Lait'. They often work well combined with smaller pompom dahlias, e.g. 'Jowey Linda', or smaller decorative dahlias, e.g. 'Edge of Joy'.

Otto's Thrill

Café au Lait

Previous page The Land Gardeners gathering dahlias in the early morning: 'Otto's Thrill', 'Santa Claus' and 'Wizard of Oz', 'Burlesca', 'Eileen' and 'Blue Bayou'.

Thomas Edison

Jowey Linda

Burlesca

White Perfection

Elma E

American Dawn

Eileen

Edge of Joy

Gerrie Hoek

Bulbs and Corms

Bulbs and corms are both underground storage units for plants: a bulb is round, comprising fleshy, scale-like layers around a central bud, while a corm is a swollen, compact stem, tending to be flatter and more solid than a bulb. They are a particularly good way of having a supply of cut flowers for picking or if you do not have the space or energy for a dedicated cut-flower garden, as they can often be planted beneath or among other flowers in your garden, or in naturalistic clumps in grassed or woodland areas, and then temporarily transplanted into pots to bring into the house.

Planting

Underplant mixed herbaceous borders with tall crown imperial fritillaries (*Fritillaria imperialis*) and Persian lily fritillaries (*Fritillaria persica*), tulips and alliums to appear in spring before the border rises around them – just remember that you will need to take care of the bulbs when lifting and dividing your perennials in autumn. For this reason, we plant narcissi in drifts along the back of the border, picking them furiously in spring, before their fading foliage is disguised by the foliage of emerging perennials. Shrubberies are also good spots for bulbs as they can stay safely tucked away from harm year after year, particularly the shade-lovers, such as delicate lily of the valley (*Convallaria majalis*) or striking martagon lilies (*Lilium martagon*).

Find areas of your garden that are quiet in spring or summer and enliven them with bulbs. We grow scillas (*Scilla siberica*) beneath our autumn-flowering raspberries and alongside our irises, creating rivers of blue through the garden in early spring. As the irises go over, the white flowers of star of Bethlehem (*Ornithogalum magnum* 'Moskou'), planted nearby, come into bloom for full summer. Meanwhile our herb garden comes alive with bees feeding on Sicilian honey garlic (*Nectaroscordum siculum*), which lasts well in a vase.

For a really low-maintenance supply of cut flowers in spring, plant camassias and narcissi in long grass. Bulbs that work well in early spring are *Narcissus* 'Thalia', the smaller 'W. P. Milner', and 'Jenny', with its reflexed petals. 'Actaea' is a good narcissus for mid-spring, followed by its later-flowering cousin, pheasant's eye daffodil (*Narcissus poeticus* var. *recurvus*), which can handle the longer grass at that time of year and flowers at the same time as the camassias.

We find that anemones and ranunculus do better in the polytunnel, which both protects them from the weather and allows us to pick them earlier in the spring.

Planting bulbs in pots is an ideal way of growing cut flowers in a small garden. Troughs of early-spring narcissi and tulips lift the spirits. In summer, we love the elegance of gladiolus 'The Bride' and regal lilies (*Lilium regale*), and in late summer Abyssinian gladiolus (*Gladiolus murielae*) provides the most unexpected flash of bright-green leaf, an unusual white flower and a heady fragrance.

For indoor bulbs in pots, plant crocuses, fritillaries, hyacinths, grape hyacinths (*Muscari*) and paperwhites (*Narcissus papyraceus*) in autumn and winter. We often grow paperwhites in a bowl, nestled among pebbles, and with just enough water to come halfway up the bulbs – they will flower away without any need for soil. Individual hyacinths, too, can be grown in special little glass hyacinth vases filled with water, to brighten your kitchen table.

Following page In-bud regal lilies (*Lilium regale*) stand in line outside the glasshouse, ready to be brought into the house to burst into flower.

Planting Depths for Bulbs

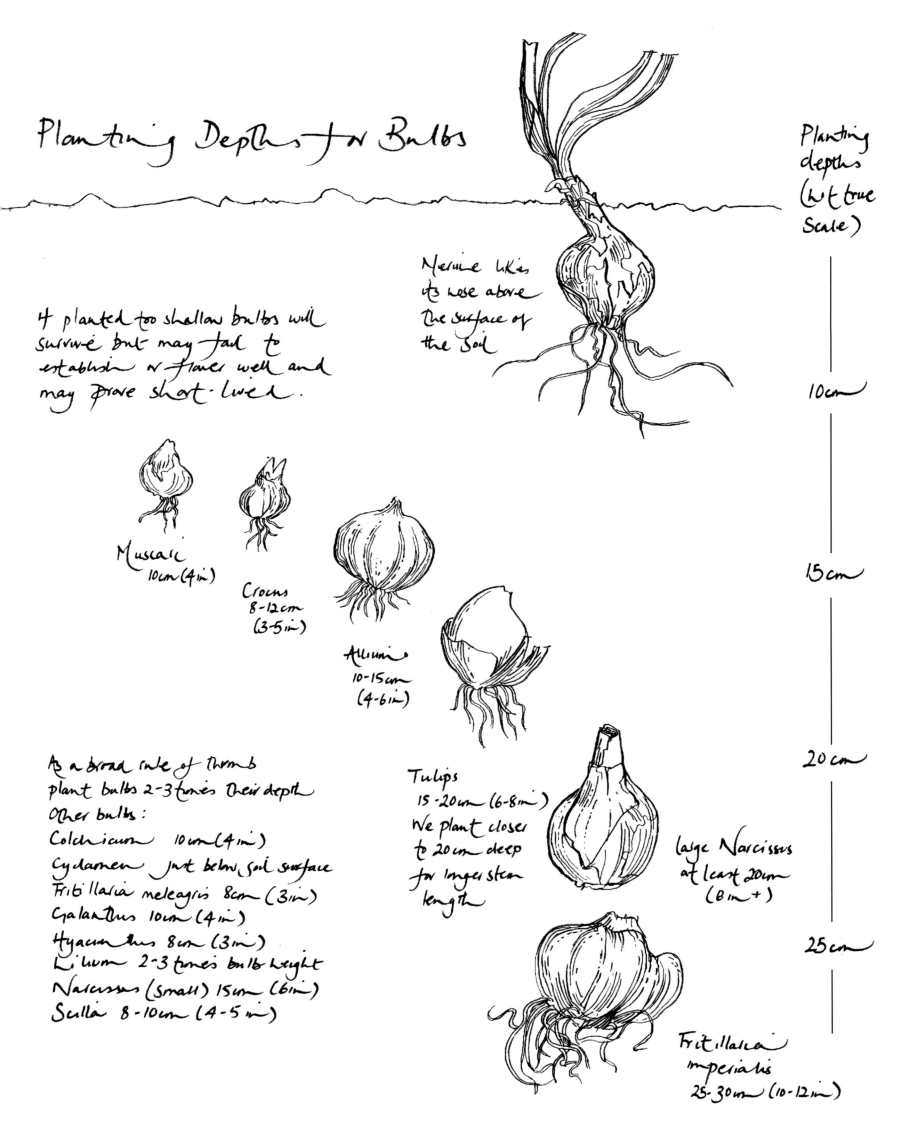

If planted too shallow bulbs will survive but may fail to establish or flower well and may prove short-lived.

Nerine likes its nose above the surface of the soil

10cm

Muscari 10cm (4in)

Crocus 8-12cm (3-5in)

Allium 10-15cm (4-6in)

15cm

As a broad rule of thumb plant bulbs 2-3 times their depth
Other bulbs:
Colchicum 10cm (4in)
Cyclamen just below soil surface
Fritillaria meleagris 8cm (3in)
Galanthus 10cm (4in)
Hyacinthus 8cm (3in)
Lilium 2-3 times bulb height
Narcissus (small) 15cm (6in)
Scilla 8-10cm (4-5in)

Tulips 15-20cm (6-8in) We plant closer to 20cm deep for longer stem length

Large Narcissus at least 20cm (8in+)

20cm

Fritillaria imperialis 25-30cm (10-12in)

25cm

221

Allium Purple
Sensation

Gladiolus
murielae

Lilium regale

Lilium
martagon

Galanthus
'S.Arnott'

Ranunculus White

Narcissus
Papyraceus Ziva

Scilla siberica

Fritillaria
imperialis

Fritillaria
meleagris

Galtonia
candicans

Convallaria
majalis

Ornithogalum
magnum MosKou

Hyacinthus
White Pearl

Muscari

Camassia leichtlinii

Crocus Jeanne
d'Arc

Narcissus poeticus
var recurvus

Tulips

When the first tulips appear, we know the circus has come to town. Striped varieties evoke all the fun of the fair, transforming our walled garden into a riot of colour and frivolity. Throughout history, rulers and growers have fallen under the magical spell of these inconspicuous bulbs, which originated from Central Asia and made their way west along the trade routes into Turkey. During the Ottoman Empire, they filled the gardens and palaces of the Turkish sultans, who were obsessed by them. And in seventeenth-century Holland, they triggered economic collapse as 'tulip mania' took hold and the bulbs were traded like stocks and shares. We, too, have thrown caution to the wind, enthralled by their charms.

Planting

Tulips like a sunny, free-draining spot in the garden and require several weeks of cold weather to flower well, so if you live in an area where the temperature does not drop down to freezing, then it would be best to buy pre-chilled bulbs. Make sure you water your tulips throughout the growing season if it is dry.

We have found an easy and effective way to grow tulips en masse. We plant in late autumn, when the ground is cold and less likely to harbour any diseases. We dig a trench 25–30 centimetres (9–12 inches) deep and 40 centimetres (16 inches) wide, then cover the base with well-rotted compost, followed by a layer of sharp sand or horticultural grit. Next, we place the tulip bulbs approximately 20 centimetres (8 inches) deep and 2 centimetres (1 inch) apart, with their pointed tips facing up, and backfill with soil. When the first shoots appear, we keep them well-watered.

Picking

This is key. When we pick tulips we do not cut them, but instead pull them from the base of the stem. This way we gain 20 centimetres (8 inches) of stem length, which really separates them from the average tulips, adding elegance and height to arrangements – our Darwin hybrids end up being impossibly long and luxurious. If the soil is wet when you are picking, the stems will be muddy, so you must rinse them well. And if the bulb pops up as you pick, then all the better – just cut the bulb off and compost it.

Lifting

To lift or not to lift? As we grow tulips on a large scale and have been afflicted by the dreaded tulip blight or fire (*Botrytis tulipae*) – a fungal disease that stunts growth and leaves grey-brown marks on the leaves and spots on the petals – we now lift our tulips when they have finished flowering. We replant them randomly in long grass or add them to our compost. This allows us to use these same beds for dahlias.

If you are growing tulips on a smaller scale or feel that lifting them is not worth the effort, choose tulips that are naturally more perennial, such as the orange 'Ballerina', green and white 'Spring Green' and velvety dark-purple 'Queen of the Night', or the Viridiflora tulips or Darwin hybrids. In flower beds, leave the dying foliage on the tulips to allow the bulb to store food for the following year before cutting them down and overplanting in high summer with short-cropping vegetables such as salad leaves.

Tulips gathered in the early morning, from the back: a bucket of tall 'Apricot Impression' and striped 'Burning Heart', a bucket of the smaller 'Apricot Pride' and, to the right, 'Apricot Parrot'. Our parrot tulips may not look so impressive in the garden, but once cut they add a swirl of fluttering ruffles to any vase.

Francoise

Twilight Princess

Apricot Impression

Carnaval de Nice

Burgundy

Mystiens Grey

Design Impression

Pink Impression

Burning Heart

Helmar

Raspberry Ripple

Flaming Club

Sorbet

Paul Scherer

Jan Reus

Apricot Pride

Spring Green

Montreux

Annuals

Annuals have a life cycle of one year. These are the plants we dream about in the depths of winter. Inexpensive to buy and to grow, they fill our buckets with cut flowers in the summer months. There is a wonderful carefree creativity about annuals. For the cost of a packet of seeds, you can grow flowers outdoors or in a pot: you can transform a spot in your garden and gather cut flowers for the house, knowing that next year you can experiment with something completely different.

Planting

If you have a small sunny patch or pot, just buy a packet of annual flower seeds and start sowing. To begin with, try growing some sweet peas (*Lathyrus odoratus*) up a fence or bamboo stakes, or sow a few nasturtium (*Tropaeolum majus*) seeds directly in the garden (they thrive in poor soil) or sprinkle love-in-a-mist (*Nigella damascena*) seeds in a sunny spot. There is really nothing more rewarding than seeing your first seeds break through the soil.

There are two types of annuals: hardy annuals, which can withstand winter frosts, and half-hardy annuals, which can't. Aside from sweet peas, nasturtiums and love-in-a-mist, we tend not to sow seeds directly in the garden, as we find they get off to a better start as seedlings. While you can begin direct-sowing hardy annuals in autumn, we prefer to start both hardy and half-hardy annuals under cover in spring, ready to plant out when the frosts are over. The only exceptions to this are the few rows of love-in-a-mist, sweet peas, bishop's flower (*Ammi majus*), bishop's weed (*Ammi visnaga*) and white laceflower (*Orlaya grandiflora*) that we sow in the polytunnel in late summer – or often actually leave to self-seed from the year before – so we have early blooms in late spring when there is a lull in flowers in the garden. Taller varieties will need staking (see page 196) as they grow.

Picking

Billowing cosmos is our late-summer and autumn staple, especially 'Purity', whose bright white flowers grow tall and continue all season – the more you pick, the more it produces. The key to cosmos is deadheading: cut cosmos can last for weeks in a vase if deadheaded, as the buds will keep opening, and we snip off dead heads in the garden as we go. You also need to keep picking sweet peas to prevent them going to seed.

The delicate silk petals of Iceland poppies (*Papaver nudicaule* 'Champagne Bubbles') flutter like butterflies among peonies.

Our favourite cosmos (*Cosmos bipinnatus*), from left to right: 'Psyche White', 'Pink Cupcake', 'Dazzler', 'Daydream', 'Purity' and 'Double Click Rose'.

Papaver
somniferum

Ammi visnaga

Antirrhinum
White Giant

Ammi majus

Papaver nudicaule
Champagne Bubbles

Scabiosa atropurpurea
White

Lathyrus odoratus
Mollie Rilstone

Lathyrus odoratus
Mrs Collier

Lathyrus odoratus
Wiltshire Ripple

Lathyrus odoratus
Windsor

Cosmos
Cupcakes

Molucella laevis

Echium vulgare
'Blue Bedder'

Nicotiana alata
Grandiflora

Didiscus coerulea
Blue Lace

Nigella papillosa
African Bride

Zinnia

Orlaya
grandiflora

Biennials

The life cycle of biennials is two years: one year they grow up, and the following year they flower and seed. They are particularly useful for providing cut flowers in late spring, when there are few flowers in the garden, and often keep flowering into the height of summer.

While we await the full crescendo of summer flowers, we pick armfuls of biennials: clouds of white honesty (*Lunaria annua* var. *albiflora*) and scented white and lavender sweet rocket (*Hesperis matronalis* var. *albiflora* and *Hesperis matronalis*); spires of white, cream and apricot foxgloves (*Digitalis purpurea* 'Sutton's Apricot'), as well as the naturalised ones (*Digitalis purpurea*); dark-maroon cow parsley (*Anthriscus sylvestris* 'Ravenswing'), with its white sea-foam on crimson-black stems; and the glorious soaring green umbels of angelica (*Angelica archangelica*). Viper's bugloss (*Echium vulgare*) is a wonderfully robust plant, with an electric-blue flower that is irresistible to bees. It grows well in hot climates and is so unfussy about growing conditions that it's often found on roadsides, but makes a good cut flower in summer mixes.

Planting and Picking

If you want to grow biennials from seed, you need to think ahead. It is a strange feeling, but just as the garden is going full-tilt in midsummer, you need to think about sowing your biennials for the following year, so they have time to establish their roots before winter sets in. We sow ours under cover and then plant them out in the autumn, but you can also direct sow them in the garden – or, if seed sowing is not your thing, buy young plants in early spring.

Once biennials are up and running, many of them will self-seed, providing you with more plants for the following year. With foxgloves, sweet rocket, angelica and honesty, we mimic nature by direct-sowing the seed in early autumn. After the foxgloves have bloomed, we let them go to seed, then pick a stem and walk around the garden, shaking out the tiny black seeds as we go. The next spring you can lift the plants and move them to where you want them.

Daucus carota
Dara

Anthriscus sylvestris
Ravenswing

Angelica
archangelica

Digitalis purpurea

Lunaria annua
var albiflora

Hesperis matronalis

Digitalis purpurea
Sutton's Apricot

Matthiola incana
Aida Apricot

Lunaria annua

Perennials

At Wardington we pick both from dedicated rows of herbaceous perennials in our cut-flower beds and from our mixed herbaceous borders in the garden. Some gardeners fear that cutting from their garden will spoil the look of their borders; however, we find that picking seems to stimulate plants to flower more and grow stronger. We clamber into the back of the borders, gathering towering pale-yellow giant scabious (*Cephalaria gigantea*) and soaring diaphanous meadow rue (*Thalictrum rochebruneanum*). We trim clouds of catmint and white and mauve valerian (*Centranthus ruber* 'Albus' and *Centranthus lecoqii*) from the terrace walls, and we stop our cars as we enter the gates to pick bistort (*Persicaria bistorta* 'Superba') from beside the drive. In late spring we rejoice when a forgotten corner of the garden heaves with the graceful arching stems of Solomon's seal (*Polygonatum* x *hybridum*), and when a client's request for tall frothing plants means we can weed out the expansionist common valerian (*Valeriana officinalis*) from our herb garden.

We have planted extra rows of some of our favourite perennials: astrantia (*Astrantia major*), which flowers all summer long; phlox (*Phlox paniculata* 'David'), for their fragrance; scabious (*Scabiosa caucasica* 'Fama' and 'Fama White'), for their nodding blue and white heads; gooseneck (*Lysimachia clethroides*), for its graceful white spikes; purple toadflax (*Linaria purpurea* 'Canon Went'), for its delicate pale-pink spires; and the lofty electric-blue bog sage (*Salvia uliginosa*), for its late-summer flowers. Rows often become beds as our obsessions grow, and we now have several beds dedicated just to delphiniums.

Planting

While perennials may not produce the same quantity of flowers as annuals, because they live for years they make perfect cut-flower plants for those less keen on sowing seeds. Plant in winter, allow them to grow and flower, then cut them back in autumn. Some perennials are more vigorous than others; after several years, you might need to lift, divide and then replant if they are growing too enthusiastically.

Delphinium 'Blue Jade' in the morning sun.

Astrantia major

Centranthus le cogii

Delphinium
Pink Ruffles

Anemone japonica
Queen Charlotte

Iris pallida
subs pallida

Linaria purpurea
Canonment

Lysimachia
clethroides

Nepeta racemosa
Amelia

Persicaria
bistorta

Alcalthaea x
suffrutescens ParKallee

Campanula
lactiflora Loddon Anna

Phlox paniculata
Mount Fuji

Salvia uliginosa

Scabiosa caucasica
perfecta Alba

Thalictrum
rochebruneanum

Valeriana
officinalis

Cephalaria
gigantea

Verbena
bonariensis

Foliage

Flowers ebb and flow throughout the year, so foliage is key. Often we use just foliage, especially evergreens over the winter months, but some greenery also makes a useful foil for flowers.

Magnolia grandiflora

Euphorbia oblongata

Euphorbia characias subsp wulfenii

Prunus laurocerasus

Polygonatum x hybridum

Petroselinum hortense Gigante di Napoli (flat leaf parsley)

Alchemilla mollis

Foeniculum vulgare

Bupleurum rotundifolium Griffithii

Rubus idaeus 'Autumn Bliss' (raspberry)

Mentha spicata (mint)

Pastinaca sativa (parsnip)

Tellima grandiflora

Cynara cardunculus

Rosmarinus officinalis (rosemary)

Climbers

Climbing plants are perfect if you do not have much space – look to your walls and fences for more opportunities for cut flowers. At Wardington, there are two old 'Lutea' banksia roses (*Rosa banksiae* 'Lutea') that flower long before any other roses in the garden. We cut sprays of their fragrant yellow flowers and also use their greenery later in the year. We can never resist the wildness of a rambling rose: the pale pink of 'Paul's Himalayan Musk', or the white flowers and hips of 'Kiftsgate'. Be warned, however, that you will need plenty of room for these, so if space is limited, turn instead to other, less vigorous roses: the repeat-flowering deep-pink 'Gertrude Jekyll' or even the once-blooming peach-pink 'Albertine'. And if you only have a shady wall, all is not lost: plant 'Madame Alfred Carrière' for its soft blush blooms, or climbing hydrangea (*Hydrangea anomala* subsp. *petiolaris*) for its airy white flowers.

We often pick from an old honeysuckle (*Lonicera periclymenum* 'Belgica') that winds its way up the iron railings of the stone steps from the lower terrace – you just won't find the intensity of colour, the scent or the character from a shop-bought equivalent. And we have just started to experiment with clematis, from the large blooms of summer-flowering clematis, such as the pale lavender 'Veronica's Choice', to the wispy ghost-like flowers of old man's beard (*Clematis vitalba*) in winter.

Planting, Feeding and Pruning

In general, climbers should be planted during the winter months, in holes that are twice the size of their rootball and enriched with compost. You should feed your climbers regularly, giving them a good mulch of compost in the autumn.

We prune our climbing roses at the end of winter, tying in the stems so that they are near-horizontal to encourage shoots along their length. The reason for this is that sap rises to the highest point of the stem, producing buds at this point, so a horizontal stem will have flower buds along its length. Once these stems have produced flowering spurs, these in turn need to be annually pruned back to approximately 10–15 centimetres (4–6 inches).

If we need to keep our ramblers under control or train them, we follow a similar technique, but mostly we are happy to let them romp away and cover walls and buildings unhindered.

Pruning clematis depends which of three groups they fall into. However, an easy rule to follow is that if your clematis flowers before midsummer, then prune lightly after flowering, as each spring it flowers on previous year's growth. However, if your clematis flowers from midsummer onwards, then hard prune each spring down to approximately 30 centimetres (1 foot) high, as it will flower on new season's growth.

Rosa Paul's Himalayan Musk

Rosa Albertine

Rosa New Dawn

Rosa Madame
Alfred Carrière

Lonicera
Periclymenum

Rosa Gertrude
Jekyll

Rosa Kiftsgate
(hips)

Rosa banksiae
lutea

Clematis tangutica

Rosa Astra
Desmond

Hydrangea
Petiolaris

Clematis Veronica's
choice

Trees and Shrubs

With its magnolias, rhododendrons and camellias, the pond walk at Wardington comes alive in spring. There is nothing shy about these spring shrubs; they are gloriously self-confident and extroverted, like those fabulous frilly swimming caps of the 1950s.

We are also expanding our collection of hydrangeas. There is a row of deep-pink mophead hydrangeas (*Hydrangea macrophylla*) by the front door, which we cut when they are in full bloom in summer, often drying them inside to tide us through the winter months. We love the plumes of paniculate hydrangeas (*Hydrangea paniculata*), the woodland feel of oak-leaved (*H. quercifolia*) varieties, the furry foliage of rough-leaved (*H. aspera*) hydrangeas and the bright lime-green pompoms of hydrangea 'Annabelle' (*Hydrangea arborescens* 'Annabelle').

In winter we find little treasures: our daphne (*Daphne odora*), which goes unnoticed for most of the year, now draws us close with its powerful scent. If nothing else, plant one near your back door to cheer you on cold, grey days and perhaps pick just one or two of its tiny fragrant flowers for your bedside table.

Planting, Feeding and Pruning

Trees and shrubs are best planted in the winter and mulched with compost and leaf mould in the autumn. Each has specific pruning requirements, which are best researched individually. In general, however, we would never clip a shrub uniformly all over, crimping it into a ball. Instead we would treat it like a fountain, cutting out long stems from the base and allowing it to arch and open freely, but rarely pruning more than a third of the plant. This gives us long, sweeping stems that we can gather and bring inside. Often we find that we are effectively 'live pruning' – cutting branches when they are in full flower, so that there is little pruning to be done beyond this.

Picking

We send sculptural branches from our magnolias to florists in London – and may even cut them while they are still in-bud, their candle-like buds protected by soft winter fur coats. We relish the hot, blowsy blooms of the rhododendrons and the intensity of the camellia flowers nestled among glossy, dark-green leaves. In late spring, it is all about blossom, armfuls and armfuls of it: cherry, apple, crab apple and quince. We bring the spring inside and relish the delicate blossom as it settles like snow around the vase.

In late spring we gather lilac (*Syringa*), and in summer flowering branches of beauty bush (*Kolkwitzia amabilis*), scented mock orange (*Philadelphus*) and deutzia (*Deutzia* x *hybrida* 'Mont Rose'). Having gathered the branches, our main concern is to prevent them from wilting by giving them a good drink and cutting their woody stems (see page 80). Mock orange can be tricky, as can lilacs and hydrangeas, so we tend to use them for events where they can shine for a night, rather than needing the stamina to last for days in a centrally heated shop or house. Having said that, if hydrangeas do not wilt, they will dry out beautifully and go on for months, often with their colour only fading a shade as they dry.

Magnolia (*Magnolia* x *soulangeana*) is one of the first trees to break the spell of winter, underplanted with bluebells (*Hyacinthoides non-scripta*), wild garlic (*Allium ursinum*), geraniums (*Geranium macrorrhizum*) and fringe cups (*Tellima grandiflora*) – all of which are great to pick.

Camellia

Cydonia oblonga

Daphne odora

Deutzia x hybrida Mont Rose

Hydrangea arborescens Annabelle

Kolkwitzia amabilis Pink Cloud

Hydrangea quercifolia

Hydrangea arborescens Pink

Hydrangea macrophylla

Magnolia x
soulangeana

Magnolia
stellata

Prunus serrulata
'Ukon'

Philadelphus

Malus

Prunus x subhirtella
Autumnalis

Rhododendron
crassum

Syringa
Charles Joly

Rhododendron
fragrantissimum

RESOURCES

BOOKS

Erin Benzakein and Julie Chai, *Floret Farm's Cut Flower Garden: Grow, Harvest and Arrange Stunning Seasonal Blooms*, Chronicle Books, 2017

Vic Brotherson, *Vintage Flowers: Choosing, Arranging, Displaying*, Kyle Books, 2011

Vic Brotherson, *Vintage Wedding Flowers*, Kyle Books, 2014

Lynn Byczynski, *The Flower Farmer*, Chelsea Green, revised edition, 2008

Shane Connolly, *Discovering the Meaning of Flowers: Love Found, Love Lost, Love Restored*, Clearview, 2017

Willow Crossley, *Flourish*, Kyle Books, 2016

Anna Day and Ellie Jauncey, *The Flower Appreciation Society: An A to Z of All Things Floral*, Sphere, 2015

Anna Pavord, *Bulb*, Mitchell Beazley, 2009

Georgina Reid and Daniel Shipp, *The Planthunter: Truth, Beauty, Chaos and Plants*, Thames & Hudson, 2018

Sarah Raven, *Grow Your Own Cut Flowers*, BBC Books, 2002

Sarah Raven, *The Cutting Garden: Growing and Arranging Garden Flowers*, Frances Lincoln, 1996

W.E. Shewell-Cooper, *Cut Flowers for the House*, Collins, 1970

Mollie Thompson, *Cut Flowers: Cultivation & Arrangement in the House*, Garden Publications, 1947

Josh Tickell, *Kiss the Ground: How the Food You Eat Can Reverse Climate Change, Heal Your Body & Ultimately Save Our World*, Atria/Enliven Books, 2017

BLOGS

Erin Benzakein, Flower Farm Journal, www.floretflowers.com/blog
The Planthunter, www.theplanthunter.com.au
Sarah Raven, www.sarahraven.com/articles

USEFUL ORGANISATIONS

UK

Biodynamic Association, www.biodynamic.org.uk
Flowers from the Farm, www.flowersfromthefarm.co.uk
Garden Organic, www.gardenorganic.org.uk
RHS, www.rhs.org.uk
Soil Association, www.soilassociation.org

US

Acres USA, www.acresusa.com
Biodynamic Association, www.biodynamics.com
Brooklyn Botanic Garden, www.bbg.org

Australia

Biodynamic Agriculture Australia, www.biodynamics.net.au
Organic Gardener, www.organicgardener.com.au

New Zealand

Biodynamics New Zealand, www.biodynamic.org.nz
Environmental Fertilisers, www.environmentalfertilisers.co.nz
Koanga Institute, www.koanga.org.nz
Organic NZ, www.organicnz.org.nz

UK SUPPLIERS

All plants and seeds

Crocus, www.crocus.co.uk
Sarah Raven, www.sarahraven.com

Seeds

Chiltern Seeds, www.chilternseeds.co.uk
Derry Watkins, www.specialplants.net

Roses

David Austin, www.davidaustinroses.co.uk
Peter Beales, www.classicroses.co.uk

Peonies

Claire Austin, www.claireaustin-hardyplants.co.uk
Kelways, www.kelways.co.uk

Dahlias

Halls of Heddon, www.hallsofheddon.com
National Dahlia Collection, www.national-dahlia-collection.co.uk

Delphiniums

Blackmore & Langdon, www.blackmore-langdon.com

Chrysanthemums

John Peace Chrysanthemums, www.johnpeace.co.uk
Woolmans, www.woolmans.com

Bulbs, corms and rhizomes (including tulips)

Avon Bulbs, www.avonbulbs.co.uk
Dix Bulbs Wholesale, www.dixexport.com
J. Parker's Wholesale, www.dutchbulbs.co.uk
Peter Nyssen, www.peternyssen.com
Woottens (for irises and perennials), www.woottensplants.com

Perennials, climbers, trees and shrubs

The Beth Chatto Gardens, www.bethchatto.co.uk
Chichester Trees and Shrubs, www.ctsplants.com
Marchants Hardy Plants (for perennials), www.marchantshardyplants.co.uk
West Kington Nurseries, www.wknurseries.co.uk

Green manures

Green Manure, www.greenmanure.co.uk
Organic Gardening Catalogue, www.organiccatalogue.com

Tools and equipment

Felco (for secateurs), www.worldoffelco.co.uk
Great Dixter, www.greatdixter.co.uk
Implementations (for copper tools), www.implementations.co.uk
Niwaki, www.niwaki.com

Flower growers and florists

Bayntun Flowers, www.bayntunflowers.co.uk
Flora Starkey, www.florastarkey.com
The Flower Appreciation Society, www.theflowerappreciationsociety.co.uk
Green and Gorgeous, www.greenandgorgeousflowers.co.uk
Scarlet & Violet, www.scarletandviolet.com
Shane Connolly, www.shaneconnolly.co.uk

US SUPPLIERS

Seeds

Floret Flowers, www.floretflowers.com
Johnny Seeds, www.johnnyseeds.com
Select Seeds, www.selectseeds.com

Roses

The Antique Rose Emporium, www.antiqueroseemporium.com
David Austin, www.davidaustinroses.com/us/shop-online
Rose Story Farm, www.rosestoryfarm.com

Peonies

Peony's Envy, www.peonysenvy.com
White Flower Farm, www.whiteflowerfarm.com

Dahlias

Dan's Dahlias, www.shop.dansdahlias.com
Swan Island Dahlias, www.dahlias.com

Delphiniums

Graceful Gardens, www.gracefulgardens.com

Chrysanthemums

King's Mums, www.kingsmums.com

Bulbs, corms and rhizomes (including tulips)

Brent and Becky's, www.brentandbeckysbullbs.com
Van Engelen, www.vanengelen.com

Perennials, climbers, trees and shrubs

Broken Arrow Nursery, www.brokenarrownursery.com
Forest Farm at Pacifica, www.forestfarm.com

Tools and equipment

A.M. Leonard, www.amleo.com
Felco, www.felco.com
Niwaki, www.niwaki.com

Flower growers and florists

3 Porch Farm, www.3porchfarm.com
Fieldwork Flowers, www.fieldworkflowers.com
Floret Flowers, www.floretflowers.com/directory
FlowerSchool New York, www.flowerschoolny.com
Saipua, www.saipua.com
Siri Thorson and Thousand Flower Farm, www.sirithorson.com
Tiny Hearts Farm, www.tinyheartsfarm.com

AUSTRALIAN SUPPLIERS

Plants and seeds

The Diggers Club, www.diggers.com.au
Eden Seeds, www.edenseeds.com.au
Lambley Nursery, www.lambley.com.au

Roses

Treloar Roses, www.treloarroses.com.au

Peonies

Spring Hill Peony Farm, www.springhillpeonyfarm.com.au

Dahlias

Country Dahlias, www.countrydahlias.com.au

Clematis

Alameda Homestead Nursery, www.ahn.com.au

Hellebores

Post Office Farm Nursery, www.postofficefarmnursery.com.au

Bulbs, corms and rhizomes (including tulips)

Red Earth Bulb Farm, www.redearthbulbs.com
Sunshine Iris, www.sunshineiris.com.au
Van Diemens Quality Bulbs, www.vdqbulbs.com.au

Perennials, climbers, trees and shrubs

Antique Perennials (wholesale only), www.antiqueperennials.com
Frogmore Gardens, www.frogmoregardens.com.au
Woodbridge Nursery, www.woodbridgenursery.com.au
Yamina Rare Plants, www.yaminarareplants.com.au

Tools and equipment

Digadoo, www.digadoo.com.au
F.D. Ryan Tools, www.fdryan.com
Grafa (for copper tools), www.grafa.com.au
Phillip & Lea, www.phillipandlea.com.au

Flower growers and florists

Cecilia Fox, www.ceciliafox.com.au
Flowers Vasette, www.flowersvasette.com.au
Lindsey Myra, www.lindseymyra.com
Oh Flora, www.ohflora.com.au

NEW ZEALAND SUPPLIERS

Seeds

Egmont Seeds, www.egmontseeds.co.nz
Kings Seeds, www.kingsseeds.co.nz

Roses

Matthews Roses, www.rosesnz.co.nz
South Pacific Roses, www.southpacificroses.co.nz
Tasman Bay Roses, www.tbr.co.nz

Peonies

New Zealand Paeony Society, www.nzpaeonies.co.nz

Dahlias and sweet peas

Dahlia Haven, www.dahliahaven.co.nz
Dr Keith Hammett, www.drkeithhammett.co.nz

Delphiniums

Dowdeswell's Delphiniums, www.delphinium.co.nz

Hydrangeas

Woodleigh Nursery, www.woodleigh.co.nz

Bulbs, corms and rhizomes (including tulips)

Amazing Iris Garden (for irises), www.irisgarden.co.nz
Aorangi Bulbs, www.aorangi.co.nz
Lilyfields, www.lilyfields.co.nz

Annuals and perennials

Seaflowers Nursery, www.seaflowersnursery.co.nz

Tools and equipment

The Garden Tool Store, www.gardentools.nz
Growing Potential, www.growingpotential.co.nz
Niwashi Gardening Tools, www.niwashi.co.nz

Flower growers and florists

Field of Roses, www.fieldofroses.co.nz
Verve Flowers, www.verveflowers.co.nz

ACKNOWLEDGEMENTS

We are incredibly grateful to everyone who has helped with this book, especially our brave and enthusiastic publisher Kirsten Abbott and talented art director Boris Bencic. Thanks also to Caitlin O'Reardon, Jessica Levine and Rachel Lucas-Craig (picture research).

We could not do any of this without our team. Thank you to our girl Friday, Michelle Harvey, who keeps our helter-skelter floral circus on the road – and who remarkably lives in Canada, which means that early afternoon we are often skyping across the Atlantic. Thank you to our brilliant gardeners Becky Craven and Rachel Lucas-Craig, and our enthusiastic volunteers Kay and Jim Black. We are hugely grateful to our team at Wardington: Edith Rabbitts, David Trafny, Lenka Freharova, Rihards Venclovs and Jason Cross. A big thank you to Katie Rees at our design studio in London for always smiling and to Sooz Lomas for working for us in Australia.

An enormous thank you to the florists who have supported us from the beginning of The Land Gardeners: Vic Brotherson from Scarlet & Violet, Shane Connolly, Flora Starkey, Anna Day and Ellie Jauncey from The Flower Appreciation Society; and to our first private client, Lulu Lytle at Soane Britain, who challenged us to produce and cut flowers from Wardington every week of the year to sit alongside her beautiful English-crafted furniture.

Above all, we are grateful to the photographers who gave up hours of their time to capture and convey the magic of flowers and Wardington – in particular Clive Nichols who lives in our village and has been so supportive, the wonderful Clare Richardson for her exquisite photographs and sage advice, and Miguel Flores-Vianna for his warmth, generosity and brilliant eye.

Thank you to the following for the images in this book: Miguel Flores-Vianna, pp. 71, 100, 140, 146, 147, 150, 151, 152–3; Andrew Montgomery/House & Garden © The Condé Nast Publications Ltd., pp. 48–9, 78; Clive Nichols, pp. 12–13, 18–19, 65, 66, 67, 87, 105, 107, 108–9, 149, 197, 218–19, 232–3, 255; Clare Richardson, pp. 2–3, 25, 27, 28, 40, 53, 62–3, 68, 72, 73, 81, 83, 84–5, 90, 92, 120–1, 122–3, 126–7, 129, 130–1, 160, 166–7, 168–9, 172, 173, 180–1, 182–3, 185, 192, 193, 200–1, 202–3, 204–5, 207, 216–17, 222–3, 239, 250–1; Hugo Rittson-Thomas, pp. 116, 124; Stephanie Fussenich, p. 21; Forbes Elworthy, pp. 76–7; Florence Charvin, p. 125; Toby Courtauld, p. 148; Britt Willoughby Dyer, p. 27 (photo of Polly Nicholson); Marcus and Jerry Harper, pp. 22–3; Daylesford Organic Cut Flower Farm, p. 23 (photo of field of cosmos); Ward/Country Life Picture Library, pp. 30–1, 34–5, 37 (1993 cover of *Country Life*); Cath Congerton, p. 37; Sonja Waites/Pulbrook & Gould, pp. 36, 38, 39; The Pease family, pp. 36, 37 (photos of Dorothy, the first Lady Wardington, and of Audrey Wardington with Sir Malcom Sargent).

Thanks also to Peter Clay and the team at Crocus, David Austin, Kelways, Claire Austin and Avon Bulbs and Chris Cocks of Taylors Clematis for their pictures. And thank you to the magic man, Stephen Johnson!

We cannot thank Emily Faccini enough for The Land Gardeners logo and for her beautiful illustrations on pages 44–5 and 221, and Boris Bencic for his letters on pages 94, 114, 138 and 158.

Thank you also to Miranda Brooks, Patrick Kinmonth, Sandra Nunnerley, Martina Mondadori Sartogo, Bunny Lytle, Dominic Amos, Charlie McCormick, Ben Pentreath, Francis Palmer, Carole Bamford, Julia Heath, Charlotte Johnstone, Paul Bangay, Belinda Handley, Felicity Rubinstein, Ike Williams, Caroline Courtauld, Anthea and Jeremy Carver, Lucy Petrie, Angelika Luebke and Urs Hildebrandt, Prue MacLeod, Alicia Drake Reece, Katie Yorke, Polly Nicholson, George Plumptre, Mary Giblin, Carolyn Ferraby, Alan Trott, Tim Scales, Phil Watts, Cath Congerton, Louise Bowman-Shaw, Willow Crossley, Anna Brown, Neves Fernandez, Emmanuel Taillard, Tim Brooks and his team, Mark Patterson, George Watts, Philip Watts, Cindy Watts, Marc Verhofstede, Steve Swatton, Emma Page, Fiona Richardson, Stuart Ellis, Charles Horner, Gay Cox, Fiona Elworthy, and Jonathan and Jennifer Horner.

Lastly, and most importantly: thank you to our families for living with our flower obsession.

Dahlia 'Café au Lait'.

First published in 2019
in the United States of America
by Thames & Hudson Inc.,
500 Fifth Avenue, New York,
New York 10110

www.thamesandhudsonusa.com

ISBN: 978-1-760-76038-0

Jacket front: Clive Nichols
Jacket back: The Land Gardeners
Author portrait: Clare Richardson

Art direction: Boris Bencic
Editing: Alison Cowan
Printed and bound in China by 1010